T. S. ELIOT

T. S. ELIOT

Colin MacCabe

© Copyright 2006 by Colin MacCabe

First published in 2006 by Northcote House Publishers Ltd, Horndon, Tavistock, Devon, PL19 9NQ, United Kingdom.
Tel: +44 (0) 1822 810066 Fax: +44 (0) 1822 810034.

British Library Cataloguing-in-Publication Data
A catalogue record for this book is available from the British Library

ISBN 0-7463-1054-4 hardcover
ISBN 0-7463-0937-6 paperback

Typeset by PDQ Typesetting, Newcastle-under-Lyme
Printed and bound in the United Kingdom

For Peter Ackroyd, the late Piers Gray and Ben Lloyd.
The better critics.

Contents

Biographical Outline

1888	26 September: T. S. Eliot is born in St. Louis, Missouri, the youngest child of Henry Ware Eliot and Charlotte Champe Eliot (née Stearns).
1896	Henry Ware Eliot builds a summer home, Eastern point, close to Gloucester, Massachussets, where Eliot will spend his childhood summers.
1898	Eliot begins schooling at Smith Academy, St. Louis.
1899	January: Edits his own magazine, *The Fireside*.
1905	Attends Milton Academy just outside Boston.
1906	Begins study for his BA at Harvard University.
1908	December: Reads Arthur Symons's *The Symbolist Movement in Literature*. Subsequently orders the *Œuvres complètes* of Jules Laforgue.
1909	BA in English Literature.
1910	MA in English Literature. Begins 'Portrait of a Lady'.
1910–11	Year spent in Paris. Attends Bergson's lectures at the Collège de France. Becomes close friends with Jean Verdenal, who will die in the slaughter of the Dardenelles. Completes 'Portrait of a Lady' and 'The Love Song of J. Alfred Prufrock'.
1911–14	Studying for a Ph.D. at Harvard with Josiah Royce. Reads F. H. Bradley's *Appearance and Reality* in 1913. Takes course on logic with Bertrand Russell in spring of 1914.
1914	Summer: Journeys through Europe before arriving in Britain just before the outbreak of war. Autumn: Begins studies to complete a thesis on Bradley at Merton College, Oxford, under Harold Joachim. 22 September: Meets Ezra Pound. Pound then reads

	Eliot's poems and announces that Eliot has 'modernized himself on his own'.
1915	Poetry published, under Pound's urgings, in both *Poetry* and *Blast*. June: Marries Vivien Haigh-Wood at Hampstead Registry Office. Neither set of parents invited to wedding. Shortly afterwards the couple moves into Bertrand Russell's flat at Russell Chambers in Bury Street, London. September: Begins teaching at High Wycombe Grammar School.
1916	January: Begins teaching at Highgate School. Starts reviewing for *New Statesman* and *International Journal of Ethics*. March: Eliot and his new wife move into a flat in 18 Crawford Mansions, just south of Baker Street. The Eliots will move frequently in the years to come, but always into flats in the west of London. April: Finishes dissertation on 'Experience and the Objects of Knowledge in the Philosophy of F. H. Bradley'.
1917	March: After a variety of teaching jobs, Eliot obtains, through his parents-in-law, a post in the Colonial and Foreign department of Lloyds Bank. June: *Prufrock and Other Observations* is published. Eliot becomes assistant editor of *The Egoist*.
1919	January: Death of Eliot's father.
1920	Publication of Eliot's major poetry from 'Prufrock' to 'Gerontion' as *Ara Vos Prec* in England and *Poems* in the United States. Publication of *The Sacred Wood*.
1921	Autumn: A nervous breakdown forces Eliot to take three months' leave from his bank job. He completes *The Waste Land*.
1922	January: Pound edits *The Waste Land*. The poem is published later in the year in both Britain and the United States. October: First issue of Eliot's journal *The Criterion* appears.
1925	Eliot leaves Lloyds and joins Faber & Gwyer (later Faber & Faber) as director. The firm publishes *Poems 1909–1925*, which includes a new poem, 'The Hollow Men'.
1927	June: Eliot is received into the Church of England. November: Takes British citizenship.
1929	September: Death of Eliot's mother.

1930	Publication of *Ash Wednesday*.
1932	Takes up the Charles Eliot Norton professorship at Harvard for the academic year 1932–33. Separates from his wife.
1934	Summer: Visits the English country house Burnt Norton with his student sweetheart Emily Hale. They had begun corresponding again in the late 1920s, and Eliot was to spend much of his holidays with Emily Hale throughout the 1930s.
1935	*Murder in the Cathedral* performed.
1936	*Collected Poems 1909–1935* includes first publication of 'Burnt Norton'.
1938	August: Vivien Eliot committed as a mental patient to Northumberland House.
1939	January: Last issue of *The Criterion* published. March: *The Family Reunion* performed. September: Britain and France declare war on Germany.
1940	Easter: publication of 'East Coker'.
1941	February: Publication of 'The Dry Salvages'.
1942	October: Publication of 'Little Gidding'.
1944	October: British publication of *Four Quartets*.
1946	After many years of nomadic living, Eliot moves into Carlyle Mansions on the Chelsea Embankment to share a flat with John Hayward.
1947	Death of Vivien Eliot.
1948	Publishes *Notes towards a Definition of Culture*. Awarded Nobel Prize and Order of Merit.
1949	*The Cocktail Party* produced. Valerie Fletcher becomes his secretary.
1953	*The Confidential Clerk* produced.
1957	Marries Valerie Fletcher. They move into Kensington Court Gardens, off High Street, Kensington.
1958	*The Elder Statesman* produced.
1965	4 January: Dies after long illness. His last word is his wife's name.

Abbreviations and References

ASG   T. S. Eliot, *After Strange Gods: a primer of modern heresy* (New York: Harcourt, Brace & Company, 1934)

ICS   T. S. Eliot, *Idea of a Christian Society* (London: Faber & Faber, 1939)

IMH   T. S. Eliot, *Inventions of the March Hare*, ed. Christopher Ricks (London: Faber & Faber, 1996)

KE   T. S. Eliot, *Knowledge and Experience in the Philosophy of F. H. Bradley* (London: Faber & Faber, 1964)

L.   T. S. Eliot, *The Letters of T. S. Eliot*, ed. Valerie Eliot (San Diego: Harcourt Brace Jovanovich, 1988)

R.   T. S. Eliot, 'Reflections on Contemporary Poetry', *The Egoist* (July 1919), 39

SE   T. S. Eliot, *Selected Essays 1917–1932* (New York: Harcourt Brace and Company, 1932)

UOM   T. S. Eliot, 'Ulysses, Order and Myth', *The Dial* (Nov. 1923), 480–3

WL   T. S. Eliot, *The Waste Land: A Facsimile and Transcript of the original drafts including the Annotations of Ezra Pound*, ed. with an intro. by Valerie Eliot (London: Faber & Faber, 1971)

All quotations from T. S. Eliot's published poetry are from *Collected Poems: 1909–1962* (London: Faber and Faber, 1963)

Preface

I have never studied or taught, except in the context of lectures on the history of the English language, the poetry of T. S. Eliot. But, of all twentieth-century poets, it is he whom I have read most often and with the most pleasure. I was thus delighted when Maud Ellmann made the suggestion that I write this book and grateful when Isobel Armstrong commissioned me.

Three friendships provided me with the necessary confidence to undertake a study for which I have little specialist qualification: Ben Lloyd, who punctuated every undergraduate day at Trinity College Cambridge with quotations from Eliot's early poems; Piers Gray, who, as a fellow graduate student at the same college, taught me the significance of Eliot's studies in philosophy; and Peter Ackroyd, a friend from both school and university, whose 1984 biography of Eliot remains for me the single most illuminating text on the poet.

This book is also the product of prolonged readings of my former student Anthony Julius's *T. S. Eliot, Anti-Semitism and Literary Form*. It was that book's reception that made me think again about the nature of Eliot's social philosophy, and it was in engagement with the compelling logic and masterly readings of Julius's book that this book took form.

The other crucial component in the writing of the book was four seminars that I conducted at the University of Pittsburgh from 2000 to 2004, the first three on Eliot and the fourth on questions of the canon. I am grateful to all the participants in the seminars, which were not only enjoyable in themselves but which also provided many of this book's emphases and opinions.

I would like to thank Stephen Heath and Cassandra Zinchini for their help in preparing the typescript for publication.

Colin MacCabe
Pittsburgh
April 2005

If jackals learnt to type and hyenas to use a pen it is certain that their work would make one think of writers like Miller, Eliot, Malraux and Sartre.

(Alexandr Fadeev, speech to the Congress of Intellectuals for Peace, August 1948, Wroclaw, Lower Silesia)

Praise be to Nero's Neptune
The Titanic sails at Dawn
Everybody's shouting
'Which side are you on?'
And Ezra Pound and T. S. Eliot
Fighting in the captain's tower
While calypso singers laugh at them
And fishermen hold flowers
Between the windows of the sea
Where lovely mermaids flow
And nobody has to think too much
About Desolation Row.

(Bob Dylan, 'Desolation Row', 1965)

Introduction

T. S. Eliot died on 4 January 1965 in London, England. At his death he was widely recognized as the greatest English poet of his time. And his most famous poem *The Waste Land* has good claim to be the greatest of poems about London. But Eliot had been born a citizen of the United States of America, and much of his intellectual formation had been in the philosophy department of Harvard University. Moreover, although he died as a communicant of the Anglican Church and is buried at East Coker in Somerset, the village of his ancestors, he had been raised in the Unitarian church of the United States.

Nearly forty years after his death he occupies a much more uncomfortable position. His conservative politics are uncongenial to an academy dominated by liberals, his belief in a Europe defined above all by its Latin culture seems to make little sense in a world in which the study of Latin is no longer central to the curriculum, and his anti-Semitism and misogyny are now less easily discounted than in the period when he was alive.

But his poetry, although very modest in quantity, remains one of the great artistic triumphs of the English language. In his ironic accounts of adolescent desire in 'The Love Song of J. Alfred Prufrock' and 'Portrait of a Lady' he performs masculine self-doubt with a pathos and wit that has yet to be surpassed in poem, book or song. But these early poems can seem like mere exercises beside the astonishing achievements of 'Gerontion' and *The Waste Land*, poems that defined a generation and that broke the mould of English verse to allow a symphony of despairing voices to bear witness to the destruction of Europe. Finally in *Four Quartets* he forged an original form and a compelling tone to hymn both religious belief and national destiny as England faced defeat at the hands of Germany. The

1

confident conclusion of *Four Quartets* that 'the fire and the rose' would be one brought his life as a poet to an end when he was only 54, almost coincidentally with the entry of the United States into the Second World War.

This poetry, although it was his chosen vocation from an early age, was not his only public achievement. Eliot never supported himself on his poetry alone and was to make his living variously as an indifferent teacher and an exemplary banker before becoming one of the most successful publishers of modern times when he joined the firm that would become famous as Faber & Faber.

Over and above the poetry and the publishing, Eliot may yet be held to have been more influential for the literary criticism that he wrote. His criticism is not much read these days; its elaborate periodic style, its elitism of reference, its dogmatic tone would make it unpalatable to any casual reader. But Eliot is perhaps the key critic in establishing a modern canon of English literature. In his championing of the Metaphysical Poets or the minor Jacobean tragedians, he was following in the footsteps of other scholars. But in his presentation of English literature from the Renaissance to the present as forming an ordered whole, he is perhaps the defining voice in the determining of a canon that was to constitute the university study of English from the end of the First World War until the 1970s in both English and American universities.

Eliot's criticism was never, however, academic. It was at the service of a social ideal of a conservative and hierarchical society that would embody the ideals of the Europe of Latin Christianity. It could be argued that Eliot's most sustained effort went not into his poetry, his criticism, or even his publishing, but into the magazine that he edited from 1922 to 1939, *The Criterion*. Quarterly for most of its existence, *The Criterion* sought to develop the kind of conservative intellectual leadership that would allow a renewed Christian Europe to grow out of the cultural suicide of the First World War. This vision was finally destroyed by the Franco-British appeasement of Hitler at Munich, and *The Criterion* ceased publication. Eliot's only major foray into social criticism after the closure of *The Criterion* is *Notes towards the Definition of Culture* – a book of unrelieved pessimism in the face of a godless and democratic age.

In his last two decades Eliot abandoned poetry, criticism and the effort to promote actively a social philosophy. He did, however, strive to reach a wider public by writing a series of verse plays that rehearsed many of the concerns of the poetry for a wider audience. But, although there are moments of great power in this drama, many of the contradictions that are held in tension in the poetry stumble rather lamely when bodied forth in a social reality as uncomfortably temporal as the poetry is timeless.

The change in Eliot's reputation is partly political, his forthright elitism challenges the general populism of both right and left, and his undoubted anti-Semitism has served as a focus to absorb the much more difficult problems that he poses for anyone committed to democratic ideals. But it is also personal. When Eliot died, it was widely known that he had spent the last decade of his life in a happy marriage with a woman many years his junior who had been his devoted secretary before she became his wife. It was also known that he had an unhappy first marriage to Vivien Haigh-Wood.[1] But Eliot was a man of considerable secrecy, and few knew the grim details of what was a long and tortured alliance, which ended with the first Mrs Eliot's commitment to a mental institution. Fewer still knew of his love for Emily Hale, who has some claim to be the muse of his late poetry, as Vivien was of *The Waste Land*. Since the 1980s there have been a number of biographies both directly about Eliot and about many of those who were his friends and acquaintances. These biographies have told us much, and much that is unflattering. Indeed, there has been a successful West End play and Oscar-nominated film *Tom and Viv*, which portrays his first wife's commitment to a mental hospital as the act of a calculating and selfish husband.

Eliot's own criticism fiercely eschewed biography. If Eliot's deep commitment to the historical sense means that he is always willing to refer to an author's relation both to his historical time and to his literary form, there is a consistent refusal to locate the mysteries of meaning in the conscious self. Eliot's criticism is above all anti-Romantic, in so far as Romanticism is understood as an emphasis on the individual self. For Eliot, both by philosophical training and by personal stance, this self is an epiphenomenon, a deluding effect of our perceptual system. The real moments of being, the moments when, to use Prufrock's terms, we hear 'the mermaids singing' – moments at which our individual consciousness participates in a wider reality cannot be named or described – although the greatest poetry does evoke them.

Any attempt to locate poetry within the individual self is to ignore the levels at which the poet cannot explain what his poetry is about, how the poetry exceeds the conscious self in the very mystery of writing, which at its best allows us to connect with the most ancient of historical pasts and to bring that past into conjunction with the most actual of contemporary presents. But if there can be no question of reducing the poetry to the biographical, it is also clear that biography can often provide a path into poetry that is consistently 'difficult'. Eliot deeply distrusted any notion of a poet expressing a 'meaning' that he understood; instead the poet works within language to provide moments of enlightenment at which the juxtaposition of words and rhythms suddenly provides access to a world that transcends the individual and links us not only to the tribe but to the species. But the route to these larger collectivities is through individual experience. And, if it is presumptuous to pretend to understand another's experience, it is possible to indicate some of the elements that compose it.

Eliot wrote, in perhaps his greatest critical essay, that the best way to understand Dante is simply to read the poetry aloud, even if your understanding of Italian is imperfect. It is advice that is just as true of his own poetry. Reading the poetry aloud is the easiest way to begin to appreciate it. And if you do not have an American accent, then you should also try to find someone who has and get them to read it to you.[2] But it is the strategy of this study to complement that direct experience of the poetry with some of its biographical contexts. These contexts do not 'explain' the poetry, but it is to be hoped that they render it less difficult, more approachable. In addition they provide perspective for a consideration of his political views.

1

Early Life

Eliot was born on 26 September 1888 in St. Louis, Missouri, the youngest child of a teacher and a merchant. His childhood was spent on the banks of the Mississippi. This great river, which was to figure so powerfully in his *Four Quartets*, had first been under the domination of the French, and it is from the French that the town gets its name. However, in 1803, Napoleon, preparing for France's titanic final struggle with the English in their 600-year war, raised much-needed cash by selling France's holdings in the United States to Jefferson. This meant that St Louis became the economic staging post for the American republic's move to dominate all the land from the Mississippi to the Pacific Ocean. Indeed the settlers already moving West had been a major reason in Jefferson's decision to purchase the Western half of the Mississippi basin. From the middle of the century this movement became one of the greatest migrations of people that the world has known. If the British Empire was established under the nostrum that trade follows the flag, the polity founded by the Pilgrim Fathers placed trade under the tutelage of the Church. It was, therefore, not surprising that some of the best and the brightest of New England's sons should choose to follow their calling by preaching on this newly established trade route. A key figure in this development of St. Louis was Henry Greenleaf Eliot, a Unitarian minister.

The most radical theological wing of the Protestantism that had developed on the north-east coast of America in the eighteenth century was Unitarianism, which denied the doctrine of the Trinity, making Jesus an exemplary man rather than a god, and which abandoned classic Calvinist doctrines of predestination in favour of an effort to live a good life on earth. Unitarianism has ancient theological ancestors and can be

5

traced back to Arius in the fourth and Arminius in the seventeenth centuries, but it gained particular force in America in the nineteenth century, when it could easily accommodate both the philological developments that made literal belief in the divinity of Jesus more difficult and the economic developments of a modern industrial society that made social improvement a pressing concern. By the time that Eliot was born, however, Unitarianism was a waning force. Its belief in Jesus as an exemplary man had made it well fitted to cope with the German scholarship that proved that the Gospels were not contemporary accounts of Jesus's life. But Unitarianism relied heavily on the argument from Design – that the complexity of man's place in the world demanded an intelligence that had wrought such an intricate design. But Darwin destroyed most simple versions of this argument, as the wonder that man could find a place in the world was replaced by the theory that he was a function of that world. If these doubts do not seem to have affected Eliot's family, the faith of the grandfather was no longer the compelling force it had been by the time the grandson reached consciousness

Henry Greenleaf Eliot saw himself as a missionary to the burgeoning Southern city of St. Louis, but he himself was of classic Yankee stock. The family name traces itself back to an Andrew Elyot who left the Somerset village of East Coker in the seventeenth century, and the Eliots figure again and again in the history of Boston and its theological disputes.

Eliot's childhood was split between St. Louis and Massachusetts, where he spent his summers in the house that his father had built for that purpose in 1896. This split between North and South a mere thirty years after the Civil War is perhaps an important part of the background to Eliot's decision, shortly before his fortieth birthday, to take British citizenship. Certainly in the year after that decision he wrote to his friend Herbert Read that he could never feel Southern because of his Yankee roots, but he could not feel a Northerner because his home had been in the South.

This split regional identity may also explain more directly what is perhaps the most mysterious feature of Eliot's whole life: his pronounced antagonism to and rejection of the New England ideology in which he had been born and raised. By the time he reached Harvard he had rejected Unitarianism, and when he became a believing Christian some twenty years later the creed he chose was High Anglican, as theologically and liturgically removed from Unitarianism as it is possible to get. Indeed, at his conversion Eliot judged Unitarianism so heterodox that it could not count as a Christian church and that he therefore needed to be baptized as an adult.

It is certainly possible, however, to read the rejection of New England in terms of gender. Eliot grew up the youngest of seven children and from the first seems to have been a 'mummy's boy', prone to illness, unable to play sports and bookish from the start. Writing was an early passion and included a family newspaper of which he was proud to style himself the editor. His mother wrote poetry, and in later life Eliot would publish her long poem on Savonarola, the fanatic friar who had urged Renaissance Florence to abandon the pleasures of trade and commerce in favour of the truths of the spirit. Writing seems for Eliot to have been the promise and guarantee of such truths of the spirit and to have been in conscious opposition to the progressive rationalism of his family faith. If to identify with his father was to make his way in the conventional world of business – and it is important to remember that Eliot was an extremely successful businessman – an identification with his mother was to reject that world in the name of art. It is important to weigh both of these aspects of Eliot – arguably the most traditional bohemian in the whole of history. The move to England may well be understood as the easiest way to live this contradiction.

Two events seem to have crystallized the process that turned a well-behaved and dutiful son of the Boston aristocracy into a poet. The first was a mystical experience at the age of 22, captured in a poem he never published, 'Silence'. The 'garrulous waves of life', are 'suddenly still' and the poet experiences a terrifying 'peace' that renders all other experience 'nothing'.

If this poem seems but a vague echo of an experience so overpowering that it marked Eliot for life, there can be no doubt that the attempt to grasp the timeless and the moment in time runs through almost all his work and will form the conclusion of his poetry in *Four Quartets*. For the moment, this experience of the unity of creation seems to have stood for a guarantee of the emptiness of the world of Boston society. If there was a writer who had analysed this world, it was the novelist Henry James. Eliot's most savage and direct dissection of this society is the poem 'Portrait of a Lady', which, apart from an indefinite article, takes its title from one of James's most famous novels.

But, if the title owes everything to an American novelist, the poem itself is the result of Eliot's second but earlier epiphany: his encounter with the French symbolist poets and particularly Jules Laforgue. In December 1908, at the age of 20, Eliot picked up Arthur Symons's *The Symbolist Movement in Literature* in a Harvard library. Symons's book deals with the movement of French poetry that takes its name from a manifesto published in *Le Figaro* on 16 September 1886, in which Jean Moreas identified a new aesthetic tendency that wanted nothing to do with realistic theatre, naturalistic novels or formally correct poetry. Symbolism covered a range of poetry from Mallarmé to Rimbaud, from Verlaine to Laforgue. What united these diverse poets was the desire to find, in the use of metaphor and image, parallels for a world that escaped the banal certainties of social life. In particular, symbolist poetry abandoned the constraints of metre and rigid form to allow the language of the poetry to find the most fundamental truths about the self.

Symbolism has a very good claim to be the first moment of modernism, the most important European aesthetic and intellectual development since Renaissance humanism. If humanism was an educational project that understood its goal as the development of the self, modernism marked a revolt against that educated self in favour of more fundamental levels of being, which escaped what was seen as the limits of consciousness. Eliot is perhaps the most conscious and intellectual of modernists, and he will explore to the full this new aesthetic, but the first moment of liberation is very specific: it is the reading of the French poet Jules Laforgue. Eliot himself talks of the moment: 'when a young writer is seized with his first passion of this sort he may be changed metamorphosed almost, within a few weeks even, from a bundle of second hand sentiments into a person' (*R.*).

No sooner was Symons's book read than Eliot sent to Paris for Laforgue's work, and over the next few months Eliot published in the Harvard student newspaper a series of poems in which one can watch a bundle of second-hand sentiments becoming a person. The second-hand sentiments are the routinized and banal thoughts about love; the person is the individual who distances himself from these thoughts through irony. It is irony that Laforgue offered to Eliot, and an ironic perspective from which the conventional emotions could be parodied. We can see his influence clearly in a very early poem, 'Nocturne', where the poetic distance allows every sentimental thought about love to be subject to the most biting irony. But, if Eliot joins Laforgue in casting scorn on the predictable emotions of a society seen as irretrievably locked into bourgeois routines, Eliot's vision is much darker than that of his French model. For Laforgue the conscious self of the bourgeois world is nothing more than a set of conventional habits, but the poet has access to the real world of the unconscious.

From early in the twentieth century onwards, the unconscious means Freud, that particular vision of how the encounter of the body and the social world creates a conscious self dependent on an incest taboo in which both incestuous wish and its interdiction are not available to consciousness. But at the beginning of the twentieth century the unconscious was available in a multitude of forms, as the full impact of Darwin's placing of man in the natural world began to be felt. For Laforgue, elaborating from the German philosopher Eduard Hartmann, it is the supreme life force – a beneficent power that only the poet or the dandy, scornful of social conditions, can access. And Laforgue's image for this is the piano – each of us embodies an individual and wonderful music, if only we could let ourselves play.

In one of his most famous formulations, Eliot said 'immature poets imitate, mature poets steal'. It is astonishing to recognize how much Eliot took from Laforgue – there is parallel after parallel, and there is no doubt that Eliot progressed from imitation to theft with great rapidity. The immature phase lasts only a few months, and Eliot republishes the poems from this phase only in a small private edition very late in life and after others had already dug them out of the Harvard student newspaper in which they had first been published. The poem that demonstrates both the astonishing influence of Laforgue

9

and how quickly Eliot reached maturity is 'Portrait of a Lady'. The poem is modelled directly on a Laforgue poem, 'Autre complainte de Lord Pierrot', a poem that we know had a particular importance for Eliot, as it was the first of Laforgue's that he had read – it is published in full by Symons. In the *Egoist* article Eliot writes very movingly, without naming Laforgue, of the 'profound kinship' that a developing poet feels for a dead poet who speaks directly to him. Laforgue's 'Other Complaint of Lord Pierrot' is a dialogue between a poet and his lover. The lover is caught in bourgeois convention; the poet has his eye on the unconscious; the final stanza calls the opposition into doubt by the hypothesis of the lover's death, which reveals that she was serious after all.

It is difficult not to believe that the feeling of 'kinship' of which Eliot speaks arose directly from his reading of this poem and particularly because of Eliot's immediate understanding of it in relation to his own situation. But when Eliot finally writes his own version of Laforgue's poem, not only is it nearly seven times as long and a strikingly vicious and misogynistic portrait, but the unconscious is not the beneficent power to which the poet appeals. Instead, it is the animal horror that bourgeois life seeks to tame. If he escapes from one, then he is caught by the other in an ironic vice that destroys his comfortable position as he articulates it.

Much of the poem is taken up with the lady's rather dull and conventional comments, which nonetheless contain just enough passive aggression to keep the young man enraged. With incredible economy, Eliot manages to tell the whole story of a year's relationship in what is a poem of just over 120 lines. We begin in winter, 'amid the smoke and fog of a December afternoon', and move through spring, 'these April sunsets', to summer, 'an August afternoon', to the final ghastly meeting of 'the October night'. Each conversation is a monologue in which the lady reveals her pathetic assumption of aesthetic and ethical superiority, the tired clichés of a totally domesticated Romanticism, to the young poet. However, the young poet is unable to fly either towards the Laforguean unconscious, which is nothing but grim savagery, or to take refuge in the social habits, which he knows to be empty. Music is the dominant metaphor; the lady evokes it in the opening lines:

10

'So intimate, this Chopin, that I think his soul
Should be resurrected only among friends
Some two or three, who will not touch the bloom
That is rubbed and questioned in the concert room.'

This oversophisticated attempt to include the poet in a relationship provokes rejection, yet the rejection is not the oceanic world of the Laforguean unconscious but the frightening world of primitive man:

a dull tom-tom begins
Absurdly hammering a prelude of its own,
Capricious monotone
That is at least one definite 'false note'.

Between the civilized embrace of high culture and the barbaric tom-tom of his instinctual reaction, the poet vainly attempts to keep his social balance. 'You will see me any morning in the park | Reading the comics and the sporting page.' But this balance is precarious, for there is a music that reminds one of desire:

Except when a street piano, mechanical and tired
Reiterates some worn-out common song
With the smell of hyacinths across the garden
Recalling things that other people have desired.
Are these ideas right or wrong?

The grandiose Laforguean piano on which being can play becomes the fleeting moment when a snatch of popular and debased culture recalls 'things that other people have desired'. But these moments cannot be turned into a coherent self, for any attempt to articulate these desires falls into the opposition between oversophistication and bestiality. The encounter with the lady is devastating to the poet, for his every attempt to place her makes clear that he cannot place himself. The poet hits rock bottom as he realizes he is like someone who, while smiling, suddenly catches sight of his reflection in a mirror – producing inevitably the sensation of falsehood: 'My self-possession gutters, we are really in the dark.'

The poem reaches a first conclusion with the recognition that we are nothing more than trained animals:

> And I must borrow every changing shape
> To find expression . . . dance, dance
> Like a dancing bear,
> Cry like a parrot, chatter like an ape.
> Let us take the air, in a tobacco trance –

But, like the tired mechanical piano, the lady's hypothetical death, stolen from Laforgue, casts even this resolution in doubt, as the lady finds her own music and the poet loses any position from which to despise her.

> Well! and what if she should die some afternoon,
> Afternoon grey and smoky, evening yellow and rose;
> Should die and leave me sitting pen in hand
> With the smoke coming down above the housetops;
> Doubtful, for a while
> Not knowing what to feel or if I understand
> Or whether wise or foolish, tardy or too soon . . .
> Would she not have the advantage, after all?
> This music is successful with a 'dying fall'
> Now that we talk of dying –
> And should I have the right to smile?

In his destruction of any position from which to assume a position of superiority, Eliot is at his most clearly anti-Romantic. Romanticism rejecting the superficiality of civilization finds authenticity in art and nature, and it is this authenticity that guarantees the authenticity of the artistic self. If that authenticity is in its turn 'civilized' and rendered false (and the lady's gushings are exactly that falsehood), then for Laforgue the unconscious offers a realm of being untouched by the poet's ironic rejection of social platitudes. But Eliot's irony is so thorough, so acidic, that it destroys any possible subjective position. This is clear in 'Portrait of a Lady', but it is much clearer in the poem that Eliot was to write after his dissection of a Bostonian hostess and that was to give the title to his first volume of poetry as well as occupying the privileged first position in that book. 'The Love Song of J. Alfred Prufrock' turns the focus from female to male speaker and thus from other to self, from object to subject. The subjectivity thus examined, the self that speaks still calls on the ironic resources offered by Laforgue, but the troubled unconscious of that self owes more to the philosopher Henri Bergson.

When he finished his MA at Harvard in the summer of 1910, Eliot determined to spend a year in Paris. If this choice was because, as Eliot was to say decades later, for him France represented poetry, for his startled and upset mother (who wrote to him, 'I can not bear to think of your being alone in Paris, the very words give me a chill' (L. 13)) it probably represented immorality and licentiousness. Eliot's determination to go to France in defiance of his mother's wishes should not be underestimated, and the pronounced change of psychic direction even found expression in a different handwriting.

Indeed, for some time Eliot seems to have seriously considered remaining in Paris and writing in French. But there was a conventional side to even this rebellious undertaking. As well as poetry there would be philosophy, in particular the lectures of Henri Bergson at the Collège de France. It is doubtful whether any philosopher of the twentieth century enjoyed the fame and renown of Bergson in 1910, and no philosopher has left so rich a literary heritage – both Proust's *Remembrance of Things Past* and Eliot's 'Prufrock' are unthinkable without his attempts to integrate modern biological thinking, and above all the theory of evolution, with a theory of consciousness. Bergson's fundamental category, vital to both Proust and Eliot, is memory. For Bergson, every memory is registered by consciousness, and we exist between two equally perilous states, one total inertia, in which we drown in the oceanic immensity of our memories, the other routinized habit, in which only those memories necessary to our conventional existence are available to consciousness. For Bergson there is an optimum state of hesitation in which we have access to a wide variety of memories that allow us to act afresh. Eliot, walking the night streets of Paris – peopled just as his mother must have feared by prostitutes – has a very different vision. In the poem 'Rhapsody on a Windy Night', the prostitute who attracts his attention does not inspire any simple lust but rather summons forth a host of memories that render any action impossible. The poet dreams of some kind of instinctual reaction, a cat licking rancid butter, a child pocketing a toy – and perhaps most powerful of all:

> And a crab one afternoon in a pool,
> An old crab with barnacles on his back,
> Gripped the end of a stick which I held him.

But these instinctual reactions are not for him. The memories that are called forth by the Parisian streets overwhelm him; it is not purposeful action informed by memories but madness that confronts the poet as 'midnight shakes the memory'. The only memory that can be trusted is controlled and habitual:

> The lamp said,
> 'Four o'clock,
> Here is the number on the door.
> Memory!
> You have the key,
> The little lamp spreads a ring on the stair.
> Mount.
> The bed is open; the tooth-brush hangs on the wall,
> Put your shoes at the door, sleep, prepare for life.'

But, as the final chilling line of the poem puts it, this is 'The last twist of the knife'. The poet resigns himself to an entirely routine life cut off from the full range of his memories, because to engage with the full range of his memories will lead, not to Bergson's 'Well- balanced mind', a man 'nicely adapted to life',[1] but, in one of the poems many horrific images, to a madman shaking a dead geranium.

It is this haunted Bergsonian self that opens 'The Love Song of J. Alfred Prufrock'. 'Let us go then, you and I,' where the 'us' is Bergson's doubled self. The self is at one and the same time caught up in the immediate perception of the world and the action that perception demands, and is also perceiving its own perception for those memories that will enable action. But this doubled perception does not open up a greater range of possible actions; it makes clear that action – and action here means both the speech act with which the lover declares himself and the act of love that will follow – is impossible. Eliot's 'us' is not a contemporaneous doubled self but a defeated 21-year-old self, a self that knows it cannot call memory to its aid, regarding with comic horror (and the poem hesitates between these two registers) the middle-aged man he is destined to become. The horror is announced in the epigraph, taken from Dante's *Inferno*. The words preface a speech by a soul in hell.

The 'patient etherised upon the table' is the Bergsonian consciousness sunk in the immensity of all its memories, as Prufrock and the reader will drown at the end, and they will drown because action is impossible: no suitable memories present themselves. The reader may be released from the poem, but Prufrock is not. As Prufrock approaches that crucial moment at which he will speak and then act with a woman, the only memories that assail him are either the half-deserted streets or the too undeserted staircase – the social desolation of the modern city and the even more desolating room where the women come and go, talking of Michelangelo. And it is women not men who inhabit these interior social spaces, these houses of intensely repressed sexuality – where the most elaborate and ornate displays of dress and conduct went together with a ban of extramarital sexual conduct of the most extreme kind. If American Puritanism did not invent the loathing of this corrupt and mortal body from which St. Paul promised we would be released, it may have a claim to have focused that loathing on female sexuality with a peculiar intensity. Eliot's father is reported to have hoped that a cure for syphilis would never be found, because otherwise it might be necessary to 'emasculate our children to keep them clean'.[2] It would be difficult to find a clearer example of what Freud was to call 'the universal tendency to debasement in the sphere of love'. This was the title of the second of three essays that Freud wrote on the topic of love in the same year as Eliot was writing 'Prufrock'. The starting point of Freud's essay is that the most common disorder for which psychoanalysts are consulted is psychic impotence, and he attempts to account for this fact in terms of the difficulty of uniting the affectionate and sensual currents of the masculine psyche. It is difficult to think of a society that had made this union more difficult than the Boston society in which Eliot had spent much of his youth and all his undergraduate life. 'Prufrock' is the song of the impotent man – the man for whom the arms 'downed with light brown hair' are as alive with an electric sexuality as they are a terrifying reminder of our bestial nature. Prufrock's inability to speak, to find the strength 'after tea and cakes and ices to force the moment to its crisis' is not simply the tortured self unable to speak its sins to anyone who lives in the human world but is also the man who would prefer to have been 'a pair of ragged claws | Scuttling across the floors of silent seas' – the crab of instinctual reaction that would allow no bar to fall across sexual desire.

15

For Freud this psychic state is not abnormal but is the inevitable consequence of the incest taboo that renders all substitute objects for the mother potentially forbidden. Freud goes so far as to say that 'psychical impotence is much more widespread than is supposed, and that a certain amount of this behaviour does in fact characterise the love of civilised man'.[3]

Eliot's conscious awareness of his situation is almost painful: he writes to his friend Conrad Aiken at the end of 1914:

> One walks about the street with one's desires, and one's refinement rises up like a wall whenever opportunity approaches. I should be better off, I sometimes think, if I had disposed of my virginity and shyness several years ago: and indeed I still think sometimes that it would be well to do so before marriage. (L. 150)

In reducing 'Prufrock' to what Freud would call its sexual aetiology, one gains some insight into its power but loses others. This is perhaps the one poem of Eliot's that it is easy to teach to undergraduates, and by report it is still much taught in American high schools. We have so far considered it from a highly gendered and historicized perspective, as the love song of a man of a particular class and period. But the poem's wide appeal cannot be explained in this way. Both boys and girls can identify with this beautiful song of adolescence, which fears that moment of declaration, not only because it will signal a fall into the flesh but much more because it will leave the self unguarded, condemned to spit out 'all the butt-ends of my days and ways' to one who may heartlessly sigh 'That is not what I meant, at all'.

And this song of adolescence is couched in the most beautiful of rhythms. The blank verse of the Elizabethan theatre is known as iambic pentameter and in its classic definition is composed of ten syllables alternating unstressed and stressed. In fact many argue that it is better understood as a four-stressed line very close to the normal rhythms of English speech. However analysed, it is the backbeat against which Prufrock plays, most obvious in those lines that we know were the first written, and that Pound urged Eliot to drop:

> No! I am not Prince Hamlet, nor was meant to be;
> Am an attendant lord, one that will do
> To swell a progress, start a scene or two,
> Advise the prince; no doubt, an easy tool . . .

16

But Eliot's purpose is not to hymn a heroic self but to sing of a hopeless one, and time and again the backbeat is broken by a turn of phrase that interrupts any too fluent melody with an individual speaking voice taken directly from Boston society. There is no solution to Prufrock's dilemma; the only women to escape the taboo of incest are imaginary sea-girls, creatures whose sexuality is untouched by the social.

The final lines leave the poet walking on the beach. There is no doubt that Eliot found many of the most intense pleasures and sensations of his youth by and on the great ocean that breaks on the Massachusetts shore. As a small boy it was crabs and rockpools; as a youth it was the excitement of pitting a small yacht against these massive forces.

Prufrock's conclusion is simple: he does not think that the mermaids, these phallic women who promise undreamt of bliss, will 'sing to me'. The final lines are the poet's, and, after Eliot's refusal of many of the easy pleasures of rhythm and rhyme, we get the most measured of lyric verses, which spell out the most bleak of conclusions: the pleasures of the mermaids will always be interrupted by the speech of our parents, and we will asphyxiate as we drown.

> I have seen them riding seaward on the waves
> Combing the white hair of the waves blown back
> When the wind blows the water white and black.
>
> We have lingered in the chambers of the sea
> By sea-girls wreathed with seaweed red and brown
> Till human voices wake us, and we drown.

The popularity of 'Prufrock' has something to do with Eliot's extreme youth when he wrote the poem. He was still only 22, so this is a poem of adolescence. It was half a century and several social revolutions later that Elvis Presley and James Dean proved that teenage angst had acquired real consumer power, but it is nonetheless easy to see 'Prufrock' as the first pop song. But few pop songs since have avoided sentimentality so assiduously nor held so mercilessly in balance the tragic and the comic as this early 'tears of a clown'.

2

From Harvard Philosophy to Literary London

The great weakness of Bergson's philosophy was that there was no place for the social in its account of consciousness. The individual and the species were the only terms; there was no account of the tribe – of the social determinations of being. When Eliot abandoned the fantasy of becoming a French poet, of dissolving his crippling American Puritanism in the brothels of Paris, he returned both to his former handwriting and to Harvard. And, in returning to Harvard, he returned not to the literature of his undergraduate degree but to its philosophy department.

Harvard philosophy had been the intellectual headquarters of Unitarianism in the early part of the nineteenth century, and it had fallen on hard times after the publication of Darwin's *Origin of Species*. But the legendary Harvard President Charles William Eliot (a distant cousin) had set out with spectacular success to revive the department, and, by the first decade of the twentieth century, Harvard's was the pre-eminent philosophy department in the country, and indeed had some claim to be the pre-eminent philosophy department in the world.[1] It had also developed a distinctive American philosophy, pragmatism. Pragmatism solved the problem of realism and idealism – whether reality was to be located in the perceived world or in the mind perceiving it – by replacing these basic terms with the notion of an active community in which meaning and truth no longer found their justification in some relation between idea and reality but in the process by which a community found agreement.

18

The great genius of pragmatism was Charles Sanders Peirce, who understood this appeal to community as distinctively American, but, by the time Eliot began his graduate work as a philosopher, Peirce had been an isolated hermit for nearly a generation and Peirce's great friend William James, who had championed his thought at Harvard, was dead. But Josiah Royce, the third great founding father of pragmatism and the one whom Eliot was to describe as the 'doyen of American philosophy', was still alive, and it was Royce who was to direct Eliot's thesis.

For Royce there were two models of a community. In the first place the community of scientists and in the second that of the early Christian Church – the congregations for whom Paul had written his epistles. There was also implicitly a third community – America. The certainties of the community of elect Protestants who had founded the New England colonies in the seventeenth century were certainties no longer as the northern states of America became the most powerful capitalist economy in the world. Capital requires labour, and the Catholic Irish who had invested Boston and New York in the aftermath of the Famine had been joined more recently by southern Italians, East European Jews and African Americans fleeing the South, to produce a society without an agreed religion or a single race. The political question to which pragmatism can in part be seen as a response was how were these disparate parts to be welded into a social whole.

Royce's own answer came in a final appeal to idealism, an absolute unity that bound the community and its interpretations into a coherent whole. James never accepted this final justification, but he did in his final years think that it might be possible to find an accommodation between his own views and Royce's in the thought of the English philosopher, F. H. Bradley. Bradley shared a coherence theory of truth with the pragmatists, but he could not have come to it from a more different route. Peirce located truth in a community interpreting itself into the future, Bradley in a past that was the only refuge from an incoherent solipsism. Bradley could not locate truth in personal experience, which even in its division into subject and object was a misleading construction, nor in an Absolute that might be logically necessary but could be known neither in its totality nor

19

in its relations. It was only a shared and coherent past that made it possible to interpret the world.

James wrote a series of letters to Bradley between 1904 and 1909 in which he begged him to link himself to the pragmatists and to become the Moses who would lead his people out of the wilderness of error.[2] When in 1913 Eliot picked F. H. Bradley for the subject of his doctoral dissertation, he was not, as it might seem in retrospect, choosing an odd byway in the last chapter of English Idealism; rather he was committing himself to the most important philosopher who might find a way to produce a theory of community that reconciled pragmatism and idealism. And, indeed, the thesis on Bradley does provide an account of truth and community that is absolutely central to the influential critical essays that Eliot was to produce immediately after finishing his dissertation in April 1916. But the critical essays were produced not in the philosophy department of Harvard, committed to producing an account of a democratic community, but in the elite literary magazines of London, deliberately eschewing wider communities for the faith of literature.

It is important to realize how that faith was for Eliot a European one. In an appreciation of Henry James that he wrote in January 1918 for *The Egoist*, of which he had become Assistant Editor, he remarked: 'It is the final perfection, the consummation of an American to become, not an Englishman, but a European – something which no born European, no person of any European nationality can become.'[3]

By the time that he wrote these words Eliot had chosen England over the native country that he was not to see again for fifteen years. He had come to Oxford in 1914 on a one-year scholarship, but by 1916 he had decided to abandon both Harvard and philosophy in favour of London and a life devoted to letters. While it would be wrong to underestimate the importance of his decision to become both an Englishman and an Anglo-Catholic in the 1920s, it is important to understand that Eliot's initial abandonment of America was not for England but for Europe, the Europe of Laforgue, more important than any English poet for his early writing, and, above all, the Europe of Dante, the great model of his later years. Indeed, Dante's political vision of a purified Holy Roman Empire is probably the closest that one can get to Eliot's ideal polity.

20

This European perspective is evident in what is probably Eliot's most significant critical essay, 'Tradition and the Individual Talent', written almost contemporaneously with the appreciation of James. Bradley's scepticism had left no place to found knowledge in experience present, past or future, but the ideal construction that we made of the present was a construction to which ideal constructions of the past were integral. Eliot had written in his thesis: 'Ideas of the past are true, not by correspondence with a real past, but by their coherence with each other and ultimately with the present moment; an idea of the past is true, we have found, by virtue of the relations among ideas' (*KE* 54). This is one of the fundamental ideas in 'Tradition and the Individual Talent', where the poet finds his meaning in the tradition that he both inherits and transforms, the tradition that Eliot describes as 'the mind of Europe' (*SE* 6).

In reading these early essays, which argue for a consistent importance of history and tradition and the centrality of an ordered community against Romanticism, Whiggery and the claims of the individual self, it would be very difficult to guess that they were the work of an American. But in the poetry that Eliot began to write at the same time, the rejection of the mind of America, incorporated in ethnically alien and sexually disgusting bodies, is all too clear. While engaged in philosophy at Harvard, Eliot had written spoof satires about an African King Bolo and his Big Black Kween. These scatological verses, which he was to produce over a number of years, and which have only recently been published (in *Inventions of the March Hare*), operate as a kind of inverse image of the impotent and retentive Prufrock. Endowed with erect cocks and loose sphincters, the inhabitants of Bololand represent a conventional fantasy of primitive peoples enjoying a direct relation to their bodies untroubled by the repressions of civilization. These crude images enter Eliot's poetry in the figure of 'Apeneck Sweeney', a compression that brings together the Southerners' loathing of the monkey-like Negro with the Bostonian fear of the priapic Irish.[4] The poem 'Sweeney Erect', which paints its disgusting picture of sexuality with colours of bestiality ('gesture of orang-outang') and mental collapse ('the epileptic on the bed'), makes clear why there is no hope for American institutions by ridiculing America's most optimistic thinker:

21

> The lengthened shadow of a man
> Is history said Emerson
> Who had not seen the silhouette
> Of Sweeney straddled in the sun.

Sweeney may be nominally Irish, but from his apeneck to his 'silhouette straddled in the sun' he is also Negroid, and it is his uncivilized sexuality, the shadow of his erect penis, that renders any American community and thus any American mind impossible. When in later life Eliot makes his own rapprochement with America, it is with the America of an idealized and imaginary past, an agrarian South in which slavery is not a problem or an issue and New England fishing communities that are ethnically and religiously homogenous. Eliot was to make a final attempt after *The Waste Land* to engage with the country of his youth in 'Sweeney Agonistes', but the abandonment of that work was also the abandonment of any attempt to be an American. That conversion to Anglo-Catholicism and naturalization as a British subject soon followed should not surprise.

But if America had to be abandoned as sexually and racially unacceptable, why did Eliot choose England from the range of European countries? In part the answer is chance: his scholarship to study Bradley took him to Oxford, and the First World War rendered Germany (which he left in August 1914 on the outbreak of the First World War), France and Italy unsuitable. There were, however, two positive reasons for his choice. The first was that England offered a literary world in which it was possible to make a mark and a living.

The crucial figure here was Ezra Pound. Pound was three years older than Eliot and a fellow American. He had studied and taught the Romance languages, and he was to develop Eliot's interest in both the Provençal poets and Dante. But above all he was a literary entrepreneur determined to seek out the best of modern writing and publish it in the small magazines with which he had contacts in both Britain and America. When he met Eliot, he had just discovered the writing of James Joyce, which he was to promote assiduously over the next decade, and he would be just as assiduous in promoting Eliot. He immediately recognized 'Prufrock' as a masterpiece and wrote to an American editor that Eliot 'has sent in the best poem I have yet had or seen from an American . . . He has actually trained himself and modernized himself on his own.'[5] It had taken Pound ten years and considerable collaboration, including work with the great Anglo-Irish poet Yeats, to develop a style that used contemporary idioms to describe contemporary reality. That someone should have freed himself from the artificial and poetic style that marked the late Victorians without collaboration seemed nothing short of astonishing to Pound. He communicated this astonishment as widely as possible and was the single most important figure in getting Eliot's early poems published in both magazine and book form. From the start Pound was also insistent that Eliot should stay in London – to go back to America was to consign oneself to provincialism. London was where literary reputations were to be made. In fact by 1920 Pound was to leave London first for France and then for Italy, but by then Eliot was more than well established.

On 29 March 1919 he wrote to his mother:

> I only write what I want to – *now* – and everyone knows that anything I do write is good. I can influence London opinion and English literature in a better way . . . There is a small and select public which regards me as the best living critic, as well as the best living poet, In England . . . I really think I have far more *influence* on English letters than any other American has ever had, unless it be Henry James. I know a great many people, but there are many more who would like to know me, and I can remain isolated and detached. (*L.* 280)

Over time Eliot was to become even more successful – at the height of his career one would have to look to Ben Jonson in the seventeenth century or Samuel Johnson in the eighteenth to find figures of comparable dominance in literary London. Indeed Eliot's position as a publisher as well as a poet, playwright, magazine editor and critic might lead one to the judgement that he surpassed even those illustrious forebears.

But if Pound and literary London are one element in Eliot's decision to stay in London, then the other was Viven Haigh-Wood and marriage:

> The awful daring of a moment's surrender
> Which an age of prudence can never retract
> By this, and this only, we have existed . . .

23

These lines from *The Waste Land*, which Eliot described as a poem that came out of the 'state of mind' occasioned by his marriage, might be read as a deliberate reference to that marriage. Certainly in Eliot's public life there is no other moment of daring to match his decision to marry Vivien Haigh-Wood in June 1915 without either of their parents' consent and a matter of weeks after he had first met her. When Eliot wrote late in life a private paper to explain a marriage that caused intense pain to both parties, he stressed his desire to abandon the life that his parents and class had mapped out for him. He stressed Pound's role too in urging him to stay and in urging Vivien to marry this young American, so that he could be saved for poetry.

But England represented more for Eliot than a literary life. It seemed also briefly to have figured a sexuality that escaped the repression attached to both Boston matrons and Parisian prostitutes. In the spring of 1914, while Eliot was still at Harvard, the English philosopher Bertrand Russell was a visiting professor. Eliot took classes with him and was also present at a Sunday garden party that was thrown in his honour by Professor Benjamin Fuller.[6] The party is the subject of a poem that Eliot published in September 1916 as 'Mr Apollinax', the name he gave to Russell in the poem. The poem describes the vitality and barely suppressed sexuality of Mr Apollinax, which are contrasted with his over-refined and over-cultivated hosts. Listening to Mr Apollinax's laughter, the poet thinks of 'Priapus in the shrubbery | Gaping at the lady in the swing' and also of the submarine world where Prufrock's mermaids swim and from which Mr Apollinax's laughter seems to come.

It may not fit dominant stereotypes to link Englishness to an emancipated sexuality. But Leonard Woolf, describing his return to England in 1911 after seven years in the colonial service, gives some sense of a genuine liberation that affected certain fractions of the English ruling class in the immediate pre-First World War years even in such matters as modes of greeting and use of Christian names:

> The social significance of using Christian instead of surnames and of kissing instead of shaking hands is curious. Their effect is greater, I think, than those who have never lived in a more formal society imagine. They produce a sense – often unconscious – of intimacy and freedom and so break down barriers to thought and feeling. It

was this feeling of greater intimacy and freedom, of the sweeping away of formalities and barriers, which I found so new and exhilarating in 1911. To have discussed some subjects or to have called a (sexual) spade a spade in the presence of Miss Strachey or Miss Stephen would seven years before have been unimaginable; here for the first time I found a much more intimate (and wider) circle in which complete freedom of thought and speech was now extended to Vanessa and Virginia, Pippa and Marjorie.[7]

Woolf is, of course, talking about the Bloomsbury Group to which Russell would introduce Eliot and Vivien after their marriage. But this social moment spread wider than one particular grouping, as Eliot made clear in a letter to Eleanor Hinkley back in the States on 24 April 1915:

I have been mostly among poets and artists, but I have also met a few ladies, and have even danced. The large hotels have dances on Saturday nights, to which one can go by paying or taking dinner there. By being admitted to two dancing parties I have met several English girls, mostly about my own age, and especially two who were very good dancers. The English style of dancing is very stiff and old fashioned, and I terrified one poor girl (she is Spanish at that) by starting to dip in my one-step. The two I mentioned are more adaptable, and caught the American style very quickly. As they are emancipated Londoners I have been out to tea or dinner with them several times, and find them quite different from anything I have known at home or here . . . They are charmingly sophisticated (even 'disillusioned') without being hardened; and I confess to taking great pleasure in seeing women smoke, though for that matter I do not know any English girls who do not. These English girls have such amusing names – I have met two named 'Phyllis' – and one named 'Vivien'. (L. 97)

Two months later he had married Vivien. If he had hoped for a release from American repression in British emancipation, he was to be bitterly disappointed. Three years later he reflected on the sexuality of cross-cultural exchanges in the only adult poem that he chose never to republish in his lifetime. The ode is a form that traditionally unites private and public emotion. Eliot had used the form in a poem that was selected to be read on graduation day at Harvard in June 1910 and that shows that Eliot had a real gift for thumping patriotic rhythm and rhyme. But the ode that he entitles 'Ode on Independence Day', 4 July 1918, could not be more different. If the poem is to link private emotion and public feeling, then the epigraph from Coriolanus makes clear that this will be, to use the poem's own words, both 'tortured' and 'tortuous'. The epigraph is taken from the speech where Coriolanus announces to Rome's deadly foes that he has abandoned a plebian and democratic Rome devoted to demagogic politics and will now use his martial skills against his mother country. Coriolanus will find that such transformations are more difficult than he thinks. Outside Rome when his mother begs him to spare his native city a broken Coriolanus in lines of astonishing power admits that it is impossible to 'stand | As if a man were author of himself | And knew no other kin'. There is no doubt that the figure of Coriolanus is of particular importance to Eliot – he occurs in the last section of *The Waste Land*; he provided the title for the most explicitly political project that he undertook. Shakespeare's play is a constant reference in Eliot's criticism. In this poem it seems to stand for the impossibility of severing oneself from one's emotional background to become the sexual author of oneself.

The first strophe finds the poet tired and misunderstood besides the stinking ('mephitic') river that we shall meet as the Thames in *The Waste Land*. The second strophe begins 'Tortured' and summons up the conjunction of the social and the animal: 'When the bridegroom smoothed his hair | There was blood upon the bed.' The final strophe begins 'Tortuous' and talks of 'fooled resentment' in the context of Perseus, the hero who slew, by using his shield as a mirror, the gorgon Medusa, whose head of writhing snakes it was impossible for any man to look on. Conventional Freudian thinking understands the Perseus myth as a dramatisation of male fear of the female genitals.

If Eliot had thought that an English bride would render him an American Perseus, then the poem has him both resentful and 'indignant'. Certainly the marriage seems to have been a sexual disaster from the start. Two weeks after they married, they dined with Russell, who had befriended Eliot after bumping into him on Oxford Street at the beginning of his English stay. In a letter to his lover Lady Ottoline Morrell, Russell wrote:

> Friday evg. I dined with my Harvard pupil Eliot & his bride. I expected her to be terrible, from his mysteriousness, but she was not so bad. She is light, a little vulgar adventurous, full of life – an artist I think he said, but I should have thought her an actress. He is

exquisite and listless, she says she married in order to stimulate him, but finds she can't do it. Obviously he married in order to be stimulated. I think she will soon be tired of him. She refuses to go to America to see his people, for fear of submarines. He is ashamed of his marriage, & very grateful if one is kind to her.[8]

Much ink has been spilled on the sexual failure of this marriage. Homosexuality, impotence and Vivien's dysmenorrhea, which led to often continuous bleeding, have all been advanced in explanations that serve only to underline our age's ludicrous belief that it is possible to parse our polymorphously perverse being into fixed parts of sex. Much better is Eliot's comment to Mary Trevelyan, the woman who was his companion for much of his middle age: 'I can't tell you, not because I don't want to but because I cannot find the words to express it.'[9] Although one probably should not ignore the chilling statement to his other companion of middle age John Hayward: 'I never lay with a woman I liked, loved or even felt any strong physical attraction to.'[10]

What is certain is that for the next decade this couple lived in an intense relationship that made them both sick (reading the catalogues of their ailments is genuinely painful) and that produced some of the greatest poetry of the twentieth century. Eliot inscribed Vivien's copy of *Poems 1909–1925* with the words 'to the only one who will fully understand them', and Vivien was Eliot's co-worker and amanuensis throughout this period. Six months after his marriage he wrote to his friend Conrad Aiken that 'I have lived through material for a score of long poems, in the last six months', and it seems that the idea of a long poem was on Eliot's mind from that time. But Eliot always found writing poetry difficult. There are few poets who produced so little over a lifetime, and every scrap of verse was repeated and worked over with patient intensity. He had suffered from a kind of block ever since he had finished 'Prufrock', and, although there are some short published poems from the period 1911–16 and some longer unpublished ones, he was afflicted by the fear that he had no more poetry in him.

Marriage to Vivien was one release, but another was accorded by recourse to French. First this meant the language itself, in which Eliot wrote a series of poems, including the first version of the 'Death by Water' sequence of *The Waste Land*. More important were the experiments he conducted in collaboration with Pound in writing quatrains modelled on the French poet Théophile Gautier. Eliot himself thought very highly of these poems. They were published in book form in 1920 as *Ara Vos Prec* and in America as *Poems 1920*, which included his 'Ode on Independence Day'. Perhaps unsurprisingly Eliot was very concerned about his mother reading this poem. He wrote to his elder brother Henry on 15 February 1920, wondering if he should cut out the page on which the ode was printed before sending his mother her copy of the book. He adds, however, that 'Sweeney among the Nightingales' and 'Burbank with a Baedeker: Bleisten with a Cigar' are 'among the best I have ever done' (*L.* 363), and no less an authority than Ackroyd calls them 'some of the most original and inventive of Eliot's work'.[11] It is true that they are full of memorable lines – 'Webster was much possessed by death | And saw the skull beneath the skin' – but the poems as a whole function as crossword puzzles of fear and loathing. *Ara Vos Prec*, like so many of Eliot's references, comes from Dante, from the *Purgatorio*, when Dante encounters the great Provençal poet Arnault. For anyone who has ever felt intimidated by Eliot's scholarship, it is a great relief to learn that Eliot initially entitled the collection *Ara Vus Prec*, his knowledge of Provençal not, at that stage, stretching to the second pronoun plural.[12] But his learning is at his most intimidating in these poems written in the third person. In the dramatic monologues that make up the vast majority of Eliot's poetry, the allusions function as further relays of meaning that the reader can follow or not, but in these poems they really are keys, the necessary condition of appreciating the poems. And the appreciation is the appreciation of hatred: hatred of women like Grishkin, hatred of proletarians like Sweeney, hatred of Jews like Bleistein. Anthony Julius has insisted that it is important to distinguish between these hatreds, that the fear and loathing that attach to the female Grishkin and the fear and envy that Sweeney provokes are different from the contempt and loathing that are visited on Bleistein. But if such distinctions are important, it is also important that they find a unity in a hatred of the body. Grishkin's 'feline smell', Sweeney 'pink from nape to base', Bleistein's 'lustreless protrusive eye': all insist on the reality of the body. Grishkin and Sweeney emphasize the body corrupted and contorted in sex, while Bleistein figures its mortality – its diseased dissolution in death. What they bear witness to in common is a physicality that appears as unbearable.

Truth to tell, it is doubtful whether these poems would be read by any but the most devoted of scholars if they had not been preceded in the original volumes by a poem in a very different form: 'Gerontion'. Like 'Prufrock', 'Gerontion' is in the form of a dramatic monologue, although the influence of Browning is now more marked. Whereas in 'Prufrock' we have a defined, if doubled, American self, in 'Gerontion' it is almost impossible to identify a character at all. The title comes from the Greek and means 'little old man', but the speaker has none of the discernible character of the earlier monologues. There can be no doubt, however, about the setting: it is Europe, the Europe of the terrible war of 1914–18 and its equally terrible peace at the Treaty of Versailles. Eliot wrote the poem in the summer of 1919 and finished it on holiday in France with Pound in August 1919, a matter of weeks after the signing of the peace treaty. 'Gerontion' is certainly the most difficult of Eliot's poems, and the power of its lines is the most resistant to any paraphrasable analysis, but there can be little doubt that it is at one level a commentary on the destruction of Europe. Indeed, one way of understanding the little old man on the verge of death is as a personification of Europe itself on the verge of extinction. 'Gerontion' is one of the old men who has not fought in the present terrible battles, but his memory ranges back to 480 BC and the 'hot gates' of Thermopylae, where the Spartan king Leonidas and his 300-strong palace guard fought to the last man to delay a Persian invasion whose success would have extinguished Europe's very beginnings in fifth-century Athens. But he is just as aware of the 'cunning passages' and 'contrived corridors' of the Peace Treaty of Versailles, which deprived Germany of over 10 per cent of its territory, including the Polish corridor that gave a reconstituted Poland access to the Baltic Sea and cut East Prussia off from the rest of Germany. It was this corridor that provided Hitler with his pretext for beginning the Second World War in September 1939.

Eliot was peculiarly aware of the devastation in central Europe, because, since March 1917, he had worked as a banker in the international section of Lloyds Bank, and after the end of the war he was charged with dealing with the reconstitution in central Europe, work that involved liaison with the Foreign Office. Although Eliot's commitment to literature was in the broadest sense social and political – the aim was 'to purify the language of the tribe' – it is very rare for him to show any interest in day-to-day politics. One of the few exceptions is the peace negotiations. Germany had surrendered in November 1918 on the basis of the American President Woodrow Wilson's 'Fourteen Points', which promised a non-punitive peace. The French in particular had other ideas, and Eliot summarizes accurately what happened in a letter to his mother:

> It is certain that at the Peace Conference the one strong figure was Clemenceau, who knew just what he wanted, and that Wilson went down utterly before European diplomacy. It is obviously a bad peace, in which the major European powers tried to get as much as they could, and appease or ingratiate as far as possible the various puppet nationalities which they have constituted and will try to dominate. That is exactly what we expected. And I believe that Wilson made a grave mistake in coming to Europe. (L. 337)

The most scathing and prescient view of the Paris conference came from John Maynard Keynes, who resigned from the British delegation and wrote *The Economic Consequences of the Peace*, which accurately predicted that the punitive reparations inflected by Clemenceau on Germany would result in another war. Although Keynes's book was not published until after 'Gerontion' had been finished, Eliot's poem was published in book form by Leonard and Virginia Woolf's Hogarth Press, and Eliot was thus an intimate of that extraordinary network known as the Bloomsbury group, of which Keynes was the most notable intellectual. It is probable that Keynes's analysis was current as conversation at the Woolfs before it was published. Certainly Eliot unusually recommended his mother to read it in a letter: 'I wonder if America realises how terrible the condition of central Europe is. I can never quite put Vienna out of my mind. And I have seen people who have been in Germany and they are most pessimistic about the future, not only of Germany, but of the world' (L. 353).

For Keynes as for Eliot, the real villain of the peace conferences was the French Prime Minister Clemenceau, an old man in his late seventies, who had prosecuted the last stages of the war with a savage intensity that he carried over to the peace negotiation. The poem begins with the cry of the Pharisees in Matthew that Jesus must produce a visible proof of his divinity. Eliot answers this with words taken from the great seventeenth-century preacher Lancelot Andrewes on the paradox of the Christ child, the Word unable to speak a word. When Christ does arrive in the poem, however, he comes as a tiger. Most commentators relate this to Blake's poem, which reflects that God's creation encompasses both the tiger and the lamb. But it is difficult to believe that anyone writing a poem in France in the summer of 1919 could use the word 'tiger' without invoking Clemenceau, whose nickname it was.

And his appearance in the poem signals a change of register as we move from a desolated Europe into a sexual encounter modelled on the ceremony of the Mass and indeterminate in the variety of its perversions. Arnault's lines 'ara vos prec' (I pray you), which gave the title to the original volume of poetry, come from the twenty-sixth canto of the *Purgatorio*, which is devoted to the lustful. Much of the canto describes those who are purging perverse sexual acts, and in both 'Geronton' and *The Waste Land* there is a deliberate and medieval refusal to treat lust as separate in its forms. This culminates in *The Waste Land* in the figure of Tiresias, both man and woman, who has 'foresuffered all | Enacted on this same divan or bed'. In 'Geronton' the passage that talks of Mr Silvero 'with caressing hands', and jumbles names, cultural references, sex and black magic together, is dense beyond explication, but Eliot told the critic F. O. Mathiessen that 'the images here are "consciously concrete"; they correspond as closely as possible to something he has actually seen and remembered'.[13]

The lines that follow this obscure sexual encounter now manage to unify both the whole history of Europe and individual sexual experience in a sequence that refuses any resolution: 'After such knowledge, what forgiveness?' The 'knowledge' is both the knowledge of what Keynes called the 'European Civil War'[14] and the carnal knowledge of a man for whom death and sex coincide as he stiffens in a rented house. Public affairs and private acts mingle together as heroism fathers unnatural vices and crime renders us virtuous. 'Geronton' makes ironic reference to John Henry Newman's *Dream of Gerontius*, where a believing Christian faces bravely the moment of death. But 'Gerontion' is neither believing nor brave. Piers Gray finds no fewer than fifteen references and allusions to the Pauline Epistles in 'Gerontion', including the identification of the soul with a building that provides the framing metaphor of the poem.[15] But Royce's ideal community of the Pauline church has dissolved into a world of international trade and culture in which profit comes from overexcited senses and pungent sauces and where sex must 'multiply variety | In a wilderness of mirrors'. As the European community dissolves in the Hall of Mirrors at the Palace of Versailles, where the doomed peace is signed, so does the coherent individual subject who can find his meaning only within a community. The poem ends in the third-person 'Thoughts of a dry brain in a dry season' no longer even unified into an 'I.' It is to read counter to the poem's disintegrating sense of person to locate these thoughts in one individual, but Tom Paulin's inspired suggestion that 'Gerontion' is Clemenceau himself finds striking confirmation in Keynes's vivid memory of the French Prime Minister at the conclusion of the negotiations that ensured that Europe's suicide could not be reversed: 'throned, in his gray gloves, on the brocade chair, dry in soul and empty of hope, very old and tired but surveying the scene with a cynical and almost impish air.'[16]

The year of the publication of 'Gerontion', Eliot gathered together his most important critical essays and published them under the title of *The Sacred Wood*. What is truly striking at this stage of Eliot's writing is the extraordinary gap between the criticism, in which there is total confidence in a tradition in which 'the mind of Europe' can accommodate both present and past, and a poetry in which both tradition and mind are dissolving into chaos. Eliot's theoretical problem at this time is how to find a method with which to identify and organise the tradition that both Bradley and his reading argue is central to any human community. This theoretical problem was genuinely acute both professionally, where his work in the foreign department of Lloyds Bank made him daily aware of the chaos of post-war central Europe, and personally, where the crisis of his own marriage was placing increasingly unbearable physical and mental suffering on both partners. This was to culminate in a full-scale breakdown at the end of 1921, when Eliot had to take three months' leave from the bank.

Eliot's problem was the simple one that, if the tradition was as vital as Eliot postulated, then it should find a coherence in more than the chance of an individual's reading. Pound put it well:

It is dawn at Jerusalem while midnight hovers above the Pillars of Hercules. All ages are contemporaneous. It is B.C., let us say, in Morocco. The Middle Ages are in Russia. The future stirs already in the minds of the few. This is especially true of literature, where the real time is independent of the apparent, and where many dead men are our grandchildren's contemporaries, while many of our contemporaries have been already gathered into Abraham's bosom, or some more fitting receptacle.

What we need is a literary scholarship, which will weigh Theocritus and Yeats with one balance, and which will judge dull dead men as inexorably as dull writers of today, and will, with equity give praise to beauty before referring to an almanack.[17]

The problem for the philosophically trained Eliot was how to justify such a 'literary scholarship'. Where was the objective account of European culture that underpinned this tradition? In particular, how to give an account of this culture that affirmed its continuing centrality in a world in which Europe had fallen apart? An early answer was provided by anti-Semitism. Hatred and persecution of the Jews are a continuous part of Europe's history, but anti-Semitism both as a term and as a significant feature of European politics takes recognizable form in the late 1870s as part of the reaction to industrial modernization. Eliot had the casual anti-Semitism of his class from early on and was famously to indulge in a poisonous Christian anti-Semitism in lectures delivered at the University of Virginia in 1933 and published the next year as *After Strange Gods*, a book that he would never allow to be republished. However anti-Semitism is central to the poetry of the *Ara Vos Prec* poems, as Anthony Julius has brilliantly demonstrated. This attachment to anti-Semitism undoubtedly had many components, and the influence of both Pound and Vivien, explicitly to align themselves with Fascist parties, is no doubt crucial. But it is important to realize that anti-Semitism at this point must also have served as a way of holding at bay the terrifying reality of Europe's dissolution.

One of the most important thinkers for Eliot from his first stay in France was Charles Maurras, whose monarchical and classical views were to underpin a particular form of ultra-right French nationalism. A virulent anti-Semite, Maurras makes clear how crucial anti-Semitism is for one who wishes to believe in a traditional view of European culture: 'Everything seems impossible, or frightfully difficult, without the providential arrival of anti-Semitism, through which all things fall into place and are simplified.'[18]

But, if it is possible to understand the theoretical place that anti-Semitism held for Eliot at this time, it is also clear that the farrago of prejudice and hatred that composes anti-Semitism could hardly sustain the developed sense of tradition that Eliot was advancing in his criticism. No more than could the 'rag-bag of Mr Pound's reading in various languages, from which one fragment after another is dragged to light and illuminated by the beauty of his phrase'. Eliot realized clearly that in the end Pound's method could be justified only as autobiography, a justification far too close to the individual Romantic sensibility from which Eliot sought to escape.[19]

But then Eliot read James Joyce's *Ulysses*. Although the novel was not to be published in its final form until 1922, Eliot was reading it from 1918 on as the assistant editor of *The Egoist*, in which early versions of some of the chapters were published. It is difficult to underestimate the effect that this novel had on Eliot. It is certain that we owe *The Waste Land* to his reading of the Irish writer. In a review of the novel published in *The Dial* Eliot wrote: 'I hold this book to be the most important expression which the present age has found; it is a book to which we are all indebted.' For Eliot, Joyce's use of the *Odyssey* for his model of a day in the life of the city of Dublin was nothing less than an important 'scientific discovery':

> In using the myth, in manipulating a continuous parallel between contemporaneity and antiquity, Mr Joyce is pursuing a method which others must pursue after him. They will not be imitators, any more than the scientist who uses the discoveries of an Einstein in pursuing his own, independent, further investigations. It is simply a way of controlling, of ordering of giving a shape and a significance to the immense panorama of futility and anarchy which is contemporary history. (*UOM* 480–3)

Eliot had been much concerned with the interpretation of religion and the question of ritual since his doctoral days at

Harvard. Indeed, he had written a very detailed and brilliant paper on the impossibility of producing any history of ritual or religion because of the impossibility of any description or interpretation of such ritual or religion not involving the observer's beliefs. If Bradley's scepticism of the impossibility of 'finite centers' communicating their experience outside an agreed tradition is accepted, then previous religions or rituals must remain incomprehensible. There was, quite simply, no possibility of the history of the meaning of religious rituals. This applied as much to the English anthropologists, such as Tylor, who imagined a pre-logical primitive man making sense of his environment according to forms of explanation that seem plausible to logical civilized man, as it did to the more sophisticated French school of Durkheim, who criticized rightly this projective form of explanation but believed none the less that it was possible to describe the facts of primitive ritual. But such a description was as dependent on modern modes of thoughts as Tylor's faulty explanation. What Joyce offered as a way out of these dilemmas was a way of reproducing myth so that it could play its function of holding disparate forms of experience together. Eliot had long distinguished between the faulty anthropologist James Frazer, who in his early work mistakenly thought that he could interpret the myth of the Hanged God, and the brilliant comparatist James Frazer, who increasingly eschewed explanation in favour of simple comparison. It was this comparative mode that Joyce brilliantly realized, as Ulysses's visit to Hades functions as the formal premiss for the funeral procession to bury Paddy Dignam at Glasnevin cemetery.

Eliot had for some years been meditating a long poem, but now his topics were not the pangs of adolescent love or the suffocating boredom of Boston. Now he was involved in a marriage of hellish intensity and a world in which European civilization was sacrificing its young men in trench warfare of unprecedented deadliness. And one of those who had died was his closest friend Jean Verdenal, the young man who had shared rooms and ideas with him in Paris in 1910–11 and with whom he had continued an intense and intimate correspondence. Many years later he was to remember as one of the simplest moment of pure pleasure in his life the evening when he had met Verdenal at dusk in the Luxembourg gardens, and his friend had come running to meet him through the spring dusk carrying a freshly torn bough of lilacs in his hands. *The Waste Land* is dedicated to him and its first lines

> April is the cruellest month, breeding
> Lilacs out of the dead land, mixing
> Memory and desire

grow lilacs out of his dead flesh. But it is a measure of the genius of Eliot's compression that these lines also carry echoes of both England's and America's first poets: the beginning of the Prologue to Chaucer's *Canterbury Tales* and Whitman's elegy on Lincoln: 'When lilacs last in the dooryard bloom'd.' One has to go back to the opening lines of *Paradise Lost*, where Milton confidently aspires to do better than Homer, Virgil and the Bible, to find a poem in English with such overweening ambition. Strangely, these were not the first lines of the typescript that Eliot confided to his friend Ezra Pound in Paris in early 1922. In the typescript the poem begins with a music-hall routine of indifferent interest. In his effort to hold the heterogeneous material of modern life together, Eliot had initially conceived of the poem as a satire. Satire, whose very etymology means variety, was the classical genre that licensed the mixing of very various matter. But Eliot's original typescript is much more obviously a satire, with each of the first four sections opening with a long pastiche. Pound allowed him to keep the Elizabethan blank verse at the beginning of the second section, but took out the music-hall routine at the beginning of 'The Burial of the Dead', the Popean satire on a fashionable London hostess at the beginning of 'The Fire Sermon' and the long sea shanty which made the 'Death by Water' section not much shorter than the other three.

It is hard to quarrel with Pound's judgement, and the publication of the original typescript in 1971 made clear that Eliot's dedication of the poem to Pound as the better poet ('il miglior fabbro') was not mere pious friendship. But Eliot may well have been willing to accept this editing because his discovery of what he took to be the Joycean method had given his poem a much more secure underpinning. In 1921 Jessie Weston had published a book entitled *From Ritual to*

Romance that took the earliest forms of vernacular European literature, the story of the Grail legend in which a knight must journey to the Chapel Perilous to discover the Cup (Grail) and the Lance that will cure the maimed and impotent Fisher King. This cure will lift the blight that lies over *The Waste Land*. Weston suggested that behind the curious imagery and themes found in the different versions of these first West European stories could be discerned older rituals in which the passage of the seasons are both imitated and ensured in the ritual sacrifice of a god.

This structure survived Pound's editing and is evident in the poem, but it is not necessary to be versed in anthropology to grasp the emphases of the poem. Georges Bataille, whose thinking grows out of meditations on anthropology and religion very similar to Eliot's, holds that the two features that distinguish men from other animals are care for the dead and the privacy of the sexual act. Thus the poem starts with the burial of the dead and the second section anatomizes the public faces of the most intimate of unions. The poem opens in a voice that mixes poetry and prophecy and that runs through the poem, being last heard four lines from the end when it tells us: 'These fragments I have shored against my ruins.' But this voice is ruptured and punctured by a medley of voices that testify to the poem's formal originality. This is not a dramatic monologue in which the poet adopts a single voice; it is a heteroglossia in which voice after voice take up the theme to produce the most beautiful and the most discordant choir in the English language. It is a testament to the psychic limits at which the poem was written and to the security that the Grail structure offered that these voices cross both gender and class.

The first eruption is the voice of an aristocratic woman speaking for the pre-1914 Europe that has died. On 2 August 1914, on the eve of war, the Foreign Secretary Lord Gray, gazing out of the Foreign Office as dusk fell, famously declared: 'the lights are going out all over Europe; we shall not see them lit again in my lifetime.' His prescience is confirmed by the pathetic voice that claims that: 'Bin gar keine Russin, stamm'aus Litauen, echt deutsch' (I am not Russian at all, I come from Lithuania, I am a real German). Lithuania was one of the states created by the Treaty of Versailles, carved out of Russia and ruled by Germans, which Eliot described in a letter to his mother of 18 December 1919 as 'puppet nationalities which (the European powers) have created and will try to dominate' (*L.* 351). It may seem daunting to find so much history compressed into one line, and that in a language not native to an English speaker, but it is completely to miss the point of the poem to think that it is necessary to grasp the full implications of the line to enjoy the poem. The voice of this frightened and rather foolish figure remembering the security of fear before the war, limited to the excitements of sledding, and the hopelessness of the current situation – 'I read, much of the night, and go south in the winter' – speaks for itself. That each line branches and radiates out into the history and culture of Europe only becomes of importance once the language has already done its work on us. In a very famous passage Eliot said that the poetry of Dante moved him long before he understood Italian properly, and he implicitly claims that this is the test of true poetry. It is certainly the test of *The Waste Land*, and most who care to read it out loud will find that it passes this test. Only then is it worth following its roots, both those signalled by Eliot in the learned and joky footnotes that he added to make up space for its book publication, and the many more that he did not.

The frightened aristocratic female voice evoking a world that has disappeared gives way to the poet as prophet, but prophet of a world without belief, where all that death yields is terror: 'I will show you fear in a handful of dust.' The failure of Christianity gives way to a comic portrait of the New Age, Madame Sosostris and her deck of Tarot cards. It is the impossibility of burying the dead, the scale of the slaughter of the Great War and the lack of beliefs that can link the living to the dead that conclude the section, as present London meets historical Carthage and the dog digs up the buried bodies of Western civilization.

In *Women Beware Women*, a play by the Elizabethan dramatist Thomas Middleton, a game of chess acts as a cover for a scene of seduction and rape. Eliot entitles the second section 'A Game of Chess' and opens it with an elaborate description of a woman's dressing table. The form is Shakespearian blank verse, and the speech continuously echoed is Enobarbus' description of Cleopatra: 'The barge she sat in, like a burnish'd throne.' Eliot's opening, however, is a description of a modern women's dressing table replete with every form of cosmetic aid and beauty product, and this satiric scene is framed by one of the most horrific myths of classical mythology: the rape of Philomel by Tereus. So that Philomel could not tell his wife, her sister, Tereus cut out her tongue. But Philomel wove the story into the tapestry that she was making, and Tereus' wife served the king a pie cooked with the flesh of his son, whom she had murdered.

This grim juxtaposition is followed by two portraits of ruined relationships, one neurotically middle class, the other explicit and demotic. Both the couple torturing themselves – in their flat 'Are you alive, or not? Is there nothing in your head?' – and the couple described in the pub – 'if you don't give it him, there's others will' – mark a sexual impasse as symbolically blighted as is the land where it is impossible to bury the dead.

The third section of the poem takes its title 'The Fire Sermon' from one of the Buddha's most famous teachings on the ravages of the desires that attach us to this world. We now find the poet by the bank of the Thames, but the echoes of Spenser and Marvell only emphasize the desolation of the present, where 'the nymphs are departed | And their friends, the loitering heirs of City directors, | Departed, have left no addresses'. The sexual bankruptcy of *The Waste Land* is made clear both by the attention of Mr Eugenides, who, in demotic French, issues an invitation to a 'weekend at the Metropole', and also by what Eliot in the notes describes as the central section of the poem, a vision of unlovely and unloved coupling, in which a house agent's clerk and a typist engage in unreproved if undesired caresses. The social and sexual loathing of this passage, which is even more evident in the unedited versions,[20] is perhaps the weakest moment of the whole poem, and it is perhaps unsurprising that Eliot has to summon Tiresias as witness to the scene:

> And I Tiresias have foresuffered all
> Enacted on this same divan or bed;
> I who have sat by Thebes below the wall
> And walked among the lowest of the dead.

In the notes Eliot identifies Tiresias as the central figure of the poem. Tiresias is significant because in classical mythology he is the only human to have experienced sex as both a man and a woman. Summoned by the king and queen of the gods to

39

determine who enjoyed the sexual act more, Tiresias enraged the queen, fatigued of her husband's importunate advances, by declaring that the woman had the better part. Blinded by the queen in her rage, Tiresias was awarded the gift of prophecy as a recompense by the king. Crucial to Eliot's poem is that the sexual act is unrewarding for both man and woman, although there are fragmentary glimpses in the city of London's churches and in an account of Queen Elizabeth and her favourite Leicester, of a different sexual and social order.

The section ends, however, with another unlovely coupling on the ever-flowing Thames, and the poet unable to hold his experience together

> 'Trams and dusty trees.
> Highbury bore me. Richmond and Kew
> Undid me. By Richmond I raised my knees
> Supine on the floor of a narrow canoe.'

> 'My feet are at Moorgate, and my heart
> Under my feet. After the event
> He wept. He promised "a new start".
> I made no comment. What should I resent?'

> 'On Margate Sands.
> I can connect
> Nothing with nothing.'

In the appeal to Buddhism and to primitive ritual, Eliot escapes from the paralysis of 'Gerontion' and the failed community of Christianity. But Christianity remains a focus of the poem, both in the Grail legend itself and also in the figure of St Augustine, who ends this passage and who preached sermons as fiery as the Buddha. The final verses of this section refer to a passage from Augustine's *Confessions*: 'To Carthage then I came, where a cauldron of unholy loves sang all about mine ears.'

Pound's most savage editing came in the fourth section, where he excised the first full three pages of typescript, which told the tale of a fishing expedition out of Cape Cod. All that is left is the story of Phlebas, both the image of man's death, but also a reference to one of the symbolic fertility rituals of a god's rebirth in which the effigy of the god that is thrown into the sea is then reclaimed as evidence of the continuity of the seasons. The final section of the poem, 'What the Thunder Said', was almost untouched by Pound – at the beginning he writes: 'OK from here on in I think.' Eliot had spent many years on the earlier sections – the line 'Come in under the shadow of this red rock' can be traced back to an unpublished poem of 1914, and Phlebas' fate had already been sketched in the French poem of 1916, 'Dans le Restaurant'. But the final section was written very quickly and almost unconsciously in Lausanne. When Eliot took sick leave from his bank, he went first to Margate, but then he travelled to Lausanne to be treated by a Dr Vittoz, and it was there that he wrote the final section in an uncharacteristic burst of inspiration, where he scarcely 'understood what I was saying'.[21]

At its simplest this section hymns the coming of rain to the dry land, the return of fertility. In this section, however, the blighted land is much more clearly identified as post-war Europe devastated by war and revolution, and the section also provides two motifs of renewal, the Grail myth and the Indian legend of what the Thunder said. Eliot had studied Sanskrit and the sacred texts of the Indian tradition at Harvard in 1912 and 1913, and he was famously to tell Stephen Spender that at the time he wrote *The Waste Land* he was almost a Buddhist. In the Indian text the single word *Da* is interpreted in three ways: *Datta* (give), *Dayadhvam* (sympathize) and *Damyata* (control). The moment of giving, 'the awful daring of a moment's surrender', is complemented by a sympathy in which Coriolanus is summoned as the image of the man entirely private to himself who must finally admit his membership of the tribe. The last continuous section of the poem links the yachting, which was a passion of Eliot's youth, to a sexual passion in which controlling hands find an obedient and joyous response.

But the poem itself does not end there, first posing the relation of the private to the public –'shall I at least set my lands in order' – before assembling a final medley of citations, fragments shored against the poet's ruin. The poem ends on a note of affirmation with 'Shantih, shantih, shantih'. In 1922 Eliot footnoted these words as follows: 'Shantih. Repeated as here, a formal ending to an Upanishad. "The Peace which passeth understanding" is a feeble translation of the content of this word'. In a reprinting of 1928 Eliot altered the final sentence of this footnote to read: 'The peace which passeth understanding is our equivalent to this word.'

3

A Dancer to God

If one reads through Eliot's letters home in the years from his marriage in 1916 to the publication of *The Waste Land* in 1922, the most recurrent subject, beating even his and Vivien's illnesses into second place, is the state of his finances. Eliot had come from a wealthy family, and his wife and their joint ailments were expensive. He was thus particularly appreciative of the patron that Pound found for him, a rich New York lawyer with an interest in literature, John Quinn. Eliot's letters to Quinn see him as unbuttoned as his four-piece suit would allow,[1] and it is interesting how definite Eliot is in this correspondence that *The Waste Land* belongs to the past. Even more striking are the terms in which he described his current project to Quinn in a letter of 26 April 1923: 'I can only say that it [Quinn's extraordinary generosity and kindness] is the greatest stimulus to me to commence the work I have in mind, which is more ambitious than anything I have ever done yet' (*WL*, pp. xxviii–xxix).

This work was never finished, but Eliot insisted that the fragments be published in all subsequent editions of his poems, where they are entitled *Sweeney Agonistes Fragments of an Aristophanic Melodrama*. This in many ways marks the culmination of Eliot's modernist experiments in an attempt to write a popular drama that would use the rhythms of the jazz age. It is a curiosity of history that St Louis produced not only America's greatest poet of the twentieth century in T. S. Eliot but also a generation later its greatest prose writer in William S. Burroughs. Burroughs's novels are populated by a cast of extraordinary characters, Dr Benway, the Impossible Kid, A.J., etc., who obviously have achieved real existence for their creator. Fresca and Mrs Porter, Eugenides and Phlebas, would seem to have had a similar reality for Eliot. His Aristophanic melodrama sees Sweeney and Doris leave the quatrains of 'Sweeney Erect' and mount the stage using a simple rhythmic language very far removed from the complicated metres and references of *The Waste Land*. Gray holds that, in *Sweeney Agonistes*, Eliot overcame a dissociation of sensibility,[2] and we might understand this comment as suggesting that the orders of thought and the orders of feeling were finding a common speech in the repetitive exchanges of the soldiers and the whores in Sweeney's establishment. Certainly Eliot finds a much more direct way of investigating both his own and his age's sexual insecurities. A great deal of moralistic ink has been spilt on Sweeney's assertion that:

> Any man might do a girl in
> Any man has to, needs to, wants to
> Once in a lifetime, do a girl in

But one can only assume that these moralists have not read Freud and in particular one of his last papers, 'Analysis Terminable and Interminable', where he meditates on a fundamental rejection in both sexes of sexual difference, a violent resentment of the other sex for the very fact of their troubling existence. For psychoanalysis, any man wants to do a girl in, and, perhaps even more unpalatably, any girl wants to return the compliment. The problem for Eliot does not seem to have been form – the seven pages reveal a new use of verse that was to provide the basis for his next phase of poetry – nor content: the fragments we have give a clear idea of the brothel setting, the narrative content and the emphasis on sex, language and, above all, isolation:

> I gotta use words when I talk to you
> But if you understand or if you don't
> That's nothing to me and nothing to you.

What Eliot lacked was a medium. Ackroyd is of the opinion that the experiment failed because 'there was no literary context for such writing from which to draw energy or inspiration . . . and he did not seem able to trust himself sufficiently with only the non-literary material derived from the ballet or the music hall'.[3] It is only in the world of parallel universes that one can imagine the meeting between Eliot and Alfred Hitchcock, arguably the twentieth century's greatest poet of the desire to do a girl in.

And, even if they had met, it would have needed another four years for the advent of talkies to have allowed Eliot, with voice over, to have solved what seemed to him the insuperable problem that the lines would need to have been spoken more quickly than the stage allowed.[4]

Eliot despised and loathed the cinema – 'continuous senseless music and continuous action too rapid for the brain to act upon' (*SE* 371) – but there can be little doubt that it was the cinema that provided the major structural principle of *The Waste Land*. While the ancient genre of satire and the more recent theories of anthropology may have provided the intellectual scaffolding for Eliot's method, both the tutor text of *Ulysses* and the poem itself proceed by the juxtaposition of scenes and images that, while theoretically possible without camera, projector and screen, was the founding principle of this new medium.[5] But if, in some Moorcockean novel, we can fantasize about the products of collaborations between Eliot and Hitchcock, the reality was that Eliot was locked into literature, and in 1925 he completed what by then looked like an inevitable process when he finally left Lloyds Bank and joined the publishing firm of Faber & Gwyer.

The year 1925 seems to have marked a real nadir in Eliot's life. Although the publishing of his *Selected Poems 1909–1925* singled him out for many as the great poet of his generation, the complete failure of his marriage made it vain to attempt to hold fast to the symbolic role of the Western hero, in particular to his masculinity. When his old friend Conrad Aiken wrote to congratulate him on the publication of this volume, he received in reply a page of *Midwives' Gazette* devoted to the forms of vaginal discharge. Eliot had underlined various words: blood, mucus, shreds of mucus, purulent offensive discharge.

Eliot had very seriously misread Joyce in his *Dial* review. For Eliot, Joyce's use of the Homeric text was a way of organizing contemporary experience according to a pattern that guaranteed order and meaning. It is just such a pattern that the Grail myth gives to *The Waste Land* – the inchoate material of which Eliot had been turning over in his mind for six years but that found form only as he read *Ulysses*. But it is interesting that Eliot's poem really does use the structure of the Grail myth and that part of its conclusion is a conventional moment of masculine domination:

> The boat responded
> Gaily, to the hand expert with sail and oar
> The sea was calm, your heart would have responded
> Gaily, when invited, beating obedient
> To controlling hands

Thus *The Waste Land* approaches to its end, but it is doubtful if Molly Bloom, the heroine of *Ulysses*, can be counted as one who waited for an invitation, still less beat obedient to controlling hands. She is an adulterous wife who no longer enjoys conventional sexual relations with her husband.

But Joyce's book, written from the position of a colonial subject during the First World War, has no wish to identify with the heroes, martial and artistic, of the dominant culture. It is no accident that Joyce chooses the name of Ulysses, Virgil's schemer of the Aeneid Book II, rather than Homer's more conventionally heroic Odysseus. Eliot could not allow himself the luxury of questioning the European tradition; his whole being was devoted to finding a version of history in which he could still function as a Christian knight without believing in Christianity. That is one way of understanding how the Grail myth functioned to organize the material of *The Waste Land* – with the very oldest European ideals of masculinity linked to even older forms of fertility ritual.

But Eliot was very aware that this organization was itself provisional and that what he required was a really new form in which he could organize his experience on a more modern footing using models of contemporary rather than classic art. However, by 1925 his marriage had broken down irretrievably and he had failed to find the contemporary form he desired. It is impossible to describe by what indirect or direct ways an individual comes to the belief that a omniscient and omnipotent God impregnated a mortal woman so that their Son could sacrifice himself in a unique historical act that redeemed Mankind from Original Sin. There can be no explanation of such a moment that is not reductive. But what can be said is that Eliot's conversion to Anglo-Catholicism in 1927 solved a number of problems for him.

First it solved the question of sex. Whatever the nature of his desires, he could not, as a married man, act on them except with his wife. If he could not be a Christian knight, then he would be a Christian monk. There is much speculation that Eliot made vows of abstinence and penitence at this time.

Secondly, it provided the absolute framework that for a moment had been promised by the coherence of literature and the European mind. The certainties of 'Tradition and the Individual Talent' in 1917 had always been troubled by a dangerous subjectivism; an omniscient God ensured that the classical order was not just a figment of one imagination. Both of these problems had been Eliot's daily bread for as long as he had been writing poetry. To those who knew him well, such as I. A. Richards and Virginia Woolf, the conversion was not surprising – Eliot's fondness for Churches and his interest in Christianity had been a much earlier shock for a circle that had abandoned Christianity. Many had read his poems as examples of a contemporary atheism and disbelief, but any who read closely could register a profound engagement with Christianity. In an unpublished poem that he wrote around 1914, and that has an early version of that terrifying line 'Come in under the shadow of this red rock', Eliot writes of a figure who gives up the Prufrockian social world of streets and rooms to become a 'dancer to God'. The conversion of 1927 had been long prepared.

It might have seemed more logical if Eliot had joined the One Holy Roman and Apostolic Church, but Roman Catholicism in both Boston and London was seen as more Irish than Roman, and if Eliot had failed to make Sweeney speak on a stage, he was unlikely to want to pray with him in a Church. Instead Eliot opted for the Anglo-Catholic wing of the Church of England.

When Elizabeth ascended to the English throne in 1558, she inherited a Church that had been devastated by Henry's original break with Rome, the Puritan radicalism of Edward VI and finally Mary's attempt to force the country back to obedience to the pope. Elizabeth's political genius was to keep the Puritans relatively happy while retaining an Episcopal system of church government that left all power of appointment of bishops in royal hands.

Gradually a theology was developed, notably by Hooker, that provided a justification for this *via media* and that combined a Catholic theology with a national Church in a national language. This Catholic theology, which became dominant under James I and Charles I, was all but eradicated in the Civil War as the Puritans took their revenge for generations of exclusion, but it remained one element of the Church of England and an element that gained renewed life and vigour from the Oxford movement in the nineteenth century. For Eliot it provided an acceptable national link with the medieval Europe to which he felt more and more drawn. Dante had been from his student years a major influence; now he became the constant point of reference, a witness to a cultural moment before Protestantism and science had dissociated thought and feeling, when the cosmos radiated Aristotelian order and Catholicism offered a coherent Church in which a finite centre might find a place.

In the same year as his conversion, Eliot became a British citizen and subsequently declared himself in the preface to his 1927 book of essays: for Lancelot Andrewes, 'classicist in literature, royalist in politics and Anglo-Catholic in religion'. If at the time it was Eliot's religious allegiance that drew most comment, in retrospect it is the political affiliation that is perhaps more surprising. For an American to declare himself a royalist is perhaps more of a repudiation of his native country than to change citizenship. But Eliot's royalism, never very evident in either his criticism or his poetry, probably is better understood as a way of distancing himself from Fascism. His two closest collaborators, Pound and Vivien, were to become active Fascists. But Fascism, with its appeal for a charismatic leader who would replace the tired bickering of democratic politics and give the modern nation a vital form, can have held little appeal for Eliot. His interest, a very American one, had never been in individual European nations but in the mind of Europe. In 1922 he had established, with the help of Lady Rothermere, a journal *The Criterion*, devoted to making his European ideal a reality. When he closed it in 1939, after Munich had ensured a Second World War that would complete the destruction of pre-1914 Europe, even Eliot realized that the mission had been quixotic.

But one should not underestimate the editorial skills that ensured contributors as eminent as Yeats and Valéry, Curtius and Hesse. Nor can one doubt the seriousness of the European commitment. *The Criterion* itself was a direct consequence of Eliot's aesthetic theories, which linked the social and the artistic in a philosophy of history taken from Hegel whereby the present both was a product of, and contained, the past. Unlike those Hegelianisms of the left that believed this process could be explained and guided, Eliot's was a sceptical idealism: the most one could cling to in the swirl of history were those established institutions that had stood the test of time. It is not surprising that *The Criterion* took Marxism so seriously in the 1930s, because from both a philosophical and a religious point of view it was the only genuine competitor with a conservative Christianity. But that Christianity, and its monarchist politics, ensured that Eliot could avoid the siren calls of Fascism.

If *Sweeney Agonistes* can be understood as the dead end of Eliot's most modernist impulses, it nonetheless yielded a new poetic method. In 1924 Eliot published as a separate poem 'Doris's Dream Song'. The method could hardly have been further from his earlier work. No complicated references, no arcane vocabulary and, perhaps most surprising of all, no backbeat of iambic pentameter. The method is above all one of repetition, the building of a poem around 'death', 'dead' and 'eyes'. Although the rhythms would become more complicated (indeed the pentameter would return as one variation) and the vocabulary more complex, Eliot had found the voice that would animate his late poetry. The most obvious influences are the sermons of Lancelot Andrewes, James I's favourite preacher. Eliot's description of Andrewes's prose style is a good guide to his own late poetry:

> It is only when we have saturated ourselves in his prose, followed the movement of his thought, that we find his examination of words terminating in the ecstasy of assent. Andrewes takes a word and derives a world from it; squeezing and squeezing the word until it yields a full juice of meaning which we should never have supposed any word to possess. (*SE* 235)

'The Hollow Men' is just this deriving of a world from very few words, but this does not make it any simpler than the earlier poetry. There is very little direct physical description, no recognizable characters such as populate *The Waste Land* and few explicit references. 'The Hollow Men' takes its epigraph from Conrad's *Heart of Darkness*, and there are clear references to the inevitable Dante as well as to Julius Caesar. But above all the poem refers to the Gunpowder Plot to blow up King James I and his Parliament in 1605 – like Caesar's assassination, a failed conspiracy. Each year on 5 November its failure is commemorated when stuffed figures representing the most famous of these conspirators, Guy Fawkes, are burnt all over England. At the most literal level, the Hollow Men, 'headpiece filled with straw', are a collection of stuffed figures waiting to burn. More generally, the poem abandons any belief in the possibility of action in this world while stopping just short of acknowledging a divine order. It also offers the most poignant recognition that religious belief finds its ground in disappointed love:

> Waking alone
> At the hour when we are
> Trembling with tenderness
> Lips that would kiss
> Form prayers to broken stone.

It is perhaps Eliot's most despairing poem, although in retrospect it is possible to read the possibility of religious salvation in the 'multifoliate rose' that appears towards the poem's end.

Eliot himself said that he thought his poetry was finished with 'The Hollow Men', and there seems to have been a long period, perhaps as long as two years, when he did not write poetry. However, shortly after his conversion he published a poem called 'Salutation' whose title evokes a passage from the *Vita Nuova*, where Dante is addressed by Beatrice 'with a salutation of such virtue that I thought then to see the world of blessedness'. The *Vita Nuova* is an account of Dante's rebirth after the devastation of exile. This rebirth finds its focus in the figure of Beatrice Portinari. It is Dante's love for Beatrice, a love that cannot be consummated, that allows him access to the love of Mary the Mother of God and then God himself. Dante's love finds its origins in the Provençal poets that he so much admired.

Developed in the castles of southern France in the twelfth century, 'courtly love' presupposed that the object of the poet's attentions, often married, could never be sexually enjoyed. This impossibility, however, intensified rather than abolished the love; indeed it was a necessary condition of a love conceived as too pure for physical realization. Eliot's Beatrice was an American woman called Emily Hale, who came from the same Boston circles as his own family. He met her in Boston while a graduate student at Harvard and acted in plays with her. She crops up in his letters when he writes from Oxford in 1914 to Conrad Aiken asking him to send her some flowers on the occasion of her appearing in a new play. Late in life Eliot wrote a note in which he said that he had been in love with Emily Hale but had been rejected before he came to Oxford. It is not clear whether Emily Hale was conscious of either the love or the rejection. There is one poem from this early period that figures a woman as loveable, the very beautiful lyric 'La Figlia che Piange' (The Girl who cries). But if the crying girl at the top of the stairs with 'her hair over her arms and her arms full of flowers' has none of the clichéd sentimentality of 'Portrait of a Lady' nor the oversophisticated ennui of Prufrock's women talking of Michaelangelo, if indeed she compels the imagination of the poet for 'many days', it is none the less clear that the poet has abandoned her and left her, as the epigraph to the poem makes explicit, 'virgo'.

We will never read the letter that Emily Hale wrote to Eliot, and that we can suppose sparked his new composition, because Eliot destroyed all her correspondence. But in 2019 his letters to her, which she deposited at Princeton University, will become available, and we will be able to read his prose reaction to the letter that she sent him in 1927 that reopened communication between them.

We know now that throughout the 1930s they saw each other regularly both in England and in America, and there seems little doubt that she is the 'lady' of 'Salutation'.

Eliot's late note suggests that his love for her was all but continuous and that he realized very soon after his marriage to Vivien that he had made a terrible mistake. If we ignore the unanswerable question as to how far Eliot was retrospectively dooming his own marriage even earlier in memory than in reality, it is certain that from 'Salutation' on he has a new female muse. And this appearance follows his first discussions with others about separation from Vivien. Although Eliot was not finally to leave his wife until 1932, the possibility that the marriage was at an end was acknowledged from 1925 on. While Eliot had a number of flirtatious relationships with English women, there seems no doubt that it was Emily Hale who occupied the place of the desired but forbidden object of courtly love, forbidden because no Anglo-Catholic could countenance the possibility of divorce. And there is poetic evidence that this love involved a reconciliation with the country of his birth. In 1927, when Eliot had been struggling with the poetic block following the failure of *Sweeney Agonistes*, Geoffrey Faber, for whose firm he had now been working for two years, suggested that he produce an occasional poem to be published as a pamphlet at Christmas. For the next four years Eliot provided such a pamphlet. The final one in this series, entitled *Marina*, was published for Christmas 1930. The title comes from Shakespeare's play *Pericles*, in which a man who has destroyed his family through jealous rage is miraculously granted a new life when he finds his long-lost daughter an unsullied virgin in a brothel. But the epigraph evokes a much more terrible recognition scene. It is taken from Seneca's play *Hercules Furens* and comprises Hercules' words as he awakens from the god-induced rage in which he has murdered his wife and children; Hercules utters the words just before he discovers what he has done. Unlike the first three Ariel poems, in which the recognition of new realities is linked to the desire for death, this poem really does promise a new beginning, and the figure of the daughter is linked to the vision of a new world – the north-east coast of America as it must have appeared to the Pilgrim Fathers and to the young sailor Eliot.

Eliot himself said that it was the Ariel poems that opened the way to his next major poem, *Ash Wednesday*. In fact it was immediately after writing the first of the Ariel poems, ' Journey of the Magi', that Eliot wrote 'Salutation', which was to become the second section of *Ash Wednesday*. As with many of Eliot's poems, *Ash Wednesday* is built out of earlier fragments, which finally combine together to produce a finished poem. Until very late in the publication process Eliot had provided the sections with headings that referred them back to Dante and above all the *Purgatorio*, but at the very last moment of the proof stage, Eliot abandoned these headings, perhaps fearing that, like the notes to *The Waste Land*, they would seem to provide an illusory 'key' to the poem. Perhaps the best guide to the poem is provided by the final section of Eliot's long essay on Dante, which he published in the year before *Ash Wednesday*. This is, for me, his finest critical essay, an introduction to his favourite poet that is also a commentary on his own work. In the final section of this essay, Eliot turns to the *Vita Nuova*, the text in which Dante discovers a new life in exile by concentrating the new meaning that he finds in a figure from his old Florentine life: Beatrice Portinari. Eliot was to write to a friend that *Ash Wednesday* 'is really a first attempt at a sketchy application of the *Vita Nuova* to modern life'.[6] The effort is to find a way of rendering personal experience in its universal aspect. The method is to combine biography and allegory in a way that confounds the very distinction of 'truth' and 'fiction'. The aim is to take the love of man and woman as a step on the way to the love of God. Eliot explicitly relates this to 'what is now called "sublimation"' (*SE* 273–5).

It is clear on reading the comments on the *Vita Nuova* that much of *Ash Wednesday* is autobiographical, and it is easy to guess that the figure of the lady is in many respects a portrait of Emily Hale, although it must say something about the confusion of Eliot's state of mind at the time that the first edition of the poem was dedicated 'To my wife', a dedication that he dropped from subsequent editions. But it would be simply perverse to read the poem biographically, even after 2019, when the letters to Emily Hale will probably make the biographical elements yet more evident. Eliot was always clear that poetry had its roots in personal experience, but the aim was always to render that experience separate from the deluding totality of the individual self. The early aim had been to find a language that would render that experience universal; *Ash Wednesday* declares that such an aim makes sense only within the context of a divine order, an order that can be glimpsed in earthly love, the figure of the Lady. The title of the poem is taken from the Christian calendar; it is the first day of Lent, traditionally inaugurating a period of fasting and abstinence and marked by a service that reminds us that we are 'dust to dust, ashes to ashes'. To attempt a paraphrase of this poem is close to impossible; words are repeated until they carry both too much meaning and too little, and much of the symbolism – the leopards, the yew trees – seems to come from an indeterminate zone where Eliot's reading and dreaming overlapped. But there is no denying the poem's beauty nor its strong message of renunciation.

Eliot has now developed a new method that has little in common with either 'Prufrock' or *The Waste Land*. Its crucial technique is repetition and its major figure paradox. The many voices, ironically balanced, of the earlier work have given way to a single voice, a voice of meditation and prayer. The force of this method can be appreciated by considering the framing phrase of the poem: 'Because I do not hope to turn again'. Its specific origin is to be found in the opening line of Cavalcanti's 'Ballad' written in exile – 'Perch'io non spero di tornar gia mai' – in which the sense is the very simple one of the exile who will never return to his homeland. Eliot, however, translates return as turn, and uses this verb again and again to invoke both the turn towards God and the turn of worldly ambition (there are echoes of the tale of Dick Whittington, to whom the bells of London said 'turn again, Whittington, Lord Mayor of London'). Indeed the context gives 'turn' a sexual meaning that is specific to the poem, for the poet is clear that, in determining not to 'turn again', he is renouncing the 'one veritable transitory power'. If the lady has not forgone her sexuality 'bellied like the fig's fruit', that sexuality is placed under the ban of incest, the 'daughter' of Marina is the 'sister, mother' of this poem. But the renunciation of worldly power in all its aspects allows the magnificent final section of the poem to recreate the homeland that had been lost:

> And the lost heart stiffens and rejoices
> In the lost lilac and the lost sea voices
> And the weak spirit quickens to rebel
> For the bent golden-rod and the lost sea smell
> Quickens to recover
> The cry of quail and the whirling plover
> And the blind eye creates
> The empty forms between the ivory gates
> And smell renews the salt savour of the sandy earth.

You do not have to know, as I did not before I wrote this book, that the 'golden-rod' is a long-stemmed yellow flower native to North America and abundant along the rocky coast of Cape Ann, to realize that Eliot is here evoking a homecoming all the more powerful because it is imaginary. And this imaginary homecoming is made possible by renunciation. It is in the awareness that he will never turn again that the poet is able to return. The poem's power is perhaps nowhere more evident than in its final line, 'And let my cry come unto Thee'. This routine Catholic response to the request 'O Lord hear my prayer' becomes in the poem the very possibility of finding an audience, the uncertain world of literary tradition replaced by the certainty of God.

It was this poem that made evident that Eliot, the supposed spokesman for an atheistic generation, had converted to Christianity, and for many his later poetry, whatever its technical accomplishment and lyric power, is vitiated by this attachment to another world. It is true that Eliot's belief in a Christianity of judgement and hell informs some of the weaker moments of the later poetry. But for the most part Eliot's Christianity appears, in his own words about Dante, 'to look to death for what life cannot give' (*SE* 235). Eliot's Christianity is only really a barrier to readers who believe that life is self-sufficient. Anyone who accepts that our lives find much of their meaning in relation to both the dead and the unborn, and that our own death is a crucial component of our life, will be untroubled by all but the most sectarian moments in Eliot's later work.

Eliot's conversion to the Church was not simply a matter of words or poems. From 1927 onwards the rituals of the Church were a constant and important factor in Eliot's day. And, over and above this, he was much concerned with the Church's spiritual and cultural mission. When Eliot came to write his final commentary for *The Criterion*, published in January 1939, he saw 1926 as the key year when it became clear that 'the intellectual and artistic output of the previous seven years had been rather the last efforts of an old world, than the first struggle of a new'.[7] The new world to which Eliot now committed himself after his conversion was not a world of European avant-garde experiment addressed to the intelligensia of Europe but a world of English theatre largely addressed to English Christians. In the early 1930s much of Eliot's creative time was devoted to *The Rock*, a pageant that offered a Christian perspective on current society, and *Murder in the Cathedral*, which used Canterbury Cathedral as the setting for a dramatic representation for the martyrdom of Thomas Becket. Indeed, from one perspective it is possible to say that, from the early 1930s to the production of *The Elder Statesman* in 1958, the majority of Eliot's creative time, if not his energy, was directed towards the theatre. The explicitly religious forms and setting of *The Rock* and *Murder in the*

Cathedral give way to a form of theatre that mixes Ibsen and Noel Coward with a large dollop of Christianized Greek drama in *The Family Reunion* (1939), and there are three further attempts in this singular genre: *The Cocktail Party* (1949), *The Confidential Clerk* (1953) and *The Elder Statesman* (1958). There can be no doubt that there are moments of great force in this theatre. The Elder Statesman's account of his wife's death, completely oblivious of her husband of many decades, is merely one of a number of moments at which the most intimate of social bonds is revealed as empty beyond imagination. But the mix of dated comedy of manners with plots of creaking complexity make these plays difficult reading.

It is a useful precept that one should not criticize writing with which one is out of sympathy. Given Eliot's prodigious talents, it cannot be ruled impossible that future generations will find more matter in this drama, but, for me, they reveal very clearly the limits of the social world that Eliot had embraced and that these plays dramatize. Eliot did not leave the world of literary London; he continued from the offices of Faber & Faber to edit many of the best poets of the next two generations. But the world he now inhabited, the world of his middle-class colleagues' families, of masculine dining clubs and clerical conventions, had taken him very far from the social and literary experimentation that Bloomsbury and Pound had offered in the aftermath of the war.

There can be little doubt that Eliot's worldly ambitions from the 1930s onwards were focused on the stage. Although his plays were not shameful failures, they were never the success that he had hoped. In the end the attempt to dramatize the most individual existential crises in the setting of his adopted English upper middle-class world did justice neither to the horror of the individual crises nor to the pleasures of the social world. But Eliot left us a much more intimate record of his time as an honorary member of his colleagues' families. Many of his holidays were spent with the families of Geoffrey Faber and Frank Morley, fellow directors of Faber & Faber, and it was for the children of these friends that Eliot used his incredible facility with rhyme and rhythm to produce *Old Possum's Book of Practical Cats*, original nursery rhymes that sketch a middle-class fantasy of the street life of London. Good Hegelian as he was, Eliot would surely have appreciated the fact that, long after his death, Andrew Lloyd Webber was to turn these poems into the libretto for the most successful play ever staged: *Cats*.

At the very beginning of *Ash Wednesday* Eliot writes that he does 'not hope to turn | Desiring this man's gift and that man's scope'. The reference is to Shakespeare's famous 'Sonnet 29', but Eliot is leaving behind not only the world of fortune and reputation but also the pentameter line of which Shakespeare is the acknowledged master in English. From now on he will seek a verse in which spoken rhythms have even more force and weight than in the earlier poetry, but these rhythms are unified by a single voice that, although it will declaim in various registers and will use the full range of English metres, will always recognizably be the voice of the poet meditating.

At the very end of his life the Buddha preached a sermon that took as its theme the lotus flower. The lotus, that most beautiful of flowers, which blooms in the most disgusting of swamps, serves as a model of how enlightenment can be produced from the most muddied of existences. It is such enlightenment that Eliot celebrates in the poem in which he first used the voice that he had sung into being in *Ash Wednesday*: 'Burnt Norton'. For us now the poem is irretrievably the first of Eliot's *Four Quartets*, but it first came into the poet's mind as a sequence that he was forced to cut from *Murder in the Cathedral*, and, even after he had developed this sequence into the long five-part poem that we now know, it was to be a further five years, when he was again forced to abandon the stage in 1940, before Eliot was to conceive it as part of a larger whole.

Burnt Norton is a manor house in Gloucestershire close to the village of Chipping Camden. In 1934 Emily Hale was staying in the village with some cousins, and Eliot was a regular visitor. They seem to have become, at least amongst Eliot's closest friends, a recognizable couple. One of their country walks took them to this house, so called because it is built on the foundations of a previous house that had burnt down.

In the play for which it was originally intended, Burnt Norton's meditation on the might-have-beens of experience come at a moment when Becket the archbishop is reminded of his youth and the alternative futures that it promised. The finished poem takes these meditations much further, turning round the endless paradox that our life, once lived, has a fixed form that is not apparent as we live it. The illumination, the lotus that arises out of the dry pool around which the poet and his companion walk, is the resolution of that paradox in which both past and possibility come together in an intensified understanding of the present. The poet contemplates both his past life – the children hiding in the bushes correspond to a moment of Eliot's St Louis childhood –and his possible one – the children that he might have had with Emily Hale. And these reflections illuminate an existence lived between the routine journeys of the underground and the flashing moment when one glimpses the flight of a kingfisher. The further paradox is that these timeless moments of illumination are themselves fleeting as we relapse into the 'waste sad time' of ordinary existence. The poem's difficulty is not a willed incomprehensibility but a consequence of the fact that the poet must evoke this moment of illumination without ever stating it. For to state it would be to fall into the fixed tenses of past, present and future, while the poem and its readers must inhabit the fluidity of meaning when experience has not resolved itself into the order of grammatical time and can be grasped in a more complex pattern.

For the first fifty years of its unquestioned position in the canon of English poetry, the biographical ground of 'Burnt Norton' was unknown to the vast majority of its readers, and the poem is not dependent for its power on the knowledge of biographical fact. But there is little question that the poem is much more approachable if one places it in the context of Eliot's failed marriage and of his relationship to Emily Hale, and that this great meditation on time and possibility gains an extra edge when one realizes the circumstances of its composition.

'Burnt Norton' was the final entry in the *Collected Poems* that Eliot published in 1936. It was not until the spring of 1940 that he returned to poetry, and when he did it was because the outbreak of war had closed the theatres. How deeply Eliot was affected by the war can be read in a short poem called 'Defence of the Islands', which he included in his *Collected Poems*, prefaced by a short statement: '*Defence of the Islands* cannot pretend to be verse, but its date – just after the evacuation from Dunkirk – and occasion have for me a significance which makes me wish to preserve it.'

57

The occasion was an exhibition in New York of photographs illustrating the British war effort; the date was Britain's darkest hour. Britain's and France's declaration of war in September 1939 had been followed by a long period of waiting for the expected terrible battles of attrition along the Maginot and Siegfried lines. But in the spring of 1940 the German high command bypassed these fortifications with a strike through Belgium, and, by June, Paris had fallen. The subsequent capitulation of the French government left Britain isolated in the struggle against the Axis powers. From that moment on, the entry of the United States into the war was the absolute priority of British policy. So Eliot's poem was one addressed to the country of his birth on behalf of the country of his choosing. Eliot evokes the various forms of Britain's defence on land, sea and air, all summoned

> to say, to the past and the future generations
> of our kin and of our speech, that we took up
> our positions, in obedience to instructions.

As in the 'hot gates' of 'Gerontion', the reference is to the pass at Thermopylae, that founding moment of Western heroism, and specifically to Leonidas' final message to the Spartans: 'we die as we have lived obedient to their commands.' But, whereas 'Gerontion' had not fought, now all are involved in the new total war of aerial bombardment and paratroop invasion. Eliot had, from the time of his conversion, played an active part in the social life of his Church. Now over 50 and subject to vertigo, he took on the duties of an air-raid warden, joining, as the poem puts it, 'those ... for whom the paths of glory are | the lanes and the streets of Britain'.

There is considerable evidence that Eliot thought of the last three Quartets as his most important contribution to the war effort. Certainly Helen Gardner, one of the first and most informed readers of the *Quartets*, talking for her generation describes them as 'the most significant literary experience of the period of the Second World War'.[8] If Eliot himself was surprised by the success of 'East Coker' when it was published in pamphlet form, he was too canny a publisher not to have been aware of his audience on both sides of the Atlantic. But, if we are to understand the force of the *Quartets*, it is not simply to their conditions of reception that we must look. After Munich, Eliot admitted to a completely new feeling, one that was not 'a criticism of the government, but the doubt of validity of a civilization' (*ICS* 64). Churchill's assumption of power in the spring of 1940 allowed those doubts to be deepened into affirmation. In the wave of revisionist history of the past generation, one feature has remained relatively untouched – the unity and solidarity of the British people as they confronted Hitler, particularly in the period from Dunkirk, and the fall of France in June 1940, to Pearl Harbor and the entry of the United States into the war in December 1941, when most rational calculation would have deemed the struggle hopeless. Perhaps the most significant cause of this national unity was that the British people were involved in a combat that was both their last great imperialist war and their heroic contribution to the international struggle against Fascism. In England in 1940, Auden's refrain from 'Spain', 'but today the struggle', chimed with an older call to arms: 'this blessed plot, this earth, this realm, this England'.[9] It was this dual nature of the political moment that produced a nation united as it had rarely, if ever, been in its history. It is this unity that is the enabling condition of *Four Quartets*, the last three of which were written in the period March 1940–September 1942.

The first step, the step towards 'East Coker', had been taken on a summer walk in 1937 when Eliot went to visit the Somerset village from which his ancestor Andrew Elyot has set out for New England in the late seventeenth century. When in early 1940 he sat down to weave a poem out of that experience, affected in part no doubt by the urgent need of closer ties with America, he took 'Burnt Norton' as his model. The symbolists had always venerated music as the greatest of the arts, because, unlike language or image, it could dispense with the misleading nature of representation in favour of a direct dramatization of being. Eliot, deeply responsive to music all his life, had used ideas of musical composition in 'Burnt Norton', and, as he began to use the same structure for 'East Coker', the idea of a quartet of poems came to him. 'Burnt Norton' had been the attempt to use the structure of a musical quartet to capture the complicated repetitions in which a whole life is figured in a moment. Now Eliot began to complicate the structure, to weave the repetitions across four poems that would not only dramatize an instant but also compose a life.

Each quartet confronts the same paradoxes of being and time, but under different aspects. If 'Burnt Norton' is the most private of the *Quartets*, then 'East Coker' is the most public, the attempt to connect the timeless moment of insight to the historical continuity marked by a bloodline and a place. And the bloodline is linked to the place by the opening sequence. Almost all Eliot's earlier poetry had turned around sexual desire, even if, as in *Ash Wednesday*, desire was figured in the form of renunciation. In *Four Quartets*, sexual desire is reduced to a simple and archaic formula taken from the writings of a sixteenth-century ancestor and placed towards the end of the opening section of 'East Coker': 'The association of man and woman | In daunsinge, signifying matrimonie | A dignified and commodious sacrament.' The conversational voice that interrupts the paradoxical lyric of the second sequence is recognizably closer to Eliot's public persona than the similar voice of 'Burnt Norton' and the avalanche of dignatories that hurtle into the dark of *Samson Agonistes* at the beginning of the third section are clearly members of Eliot's social world. If the religious emphasis of 'Burnt Norton' was Buddhist, 'East Coker' is Christian. The moment of illumination comes from the 'negative way' of St John of the Cross, and the short lyric of the fourth section makes clear the reality of the sacrificial meal of God's Body and Blood. At the centre of 'East Coker' is the rejection of any notion of maturity as a settled sense of identity – 'every moment is a new and shocking | Valuation of all we have been' – and the determination to move 'into another intensity | For a further union, a deeper communion'. The poem opens with the statement 'In my beginning is my end', tracing himself back to a vanished England, and closes with the reversal, 'In my end is my beginning', the affirmation of the power of the present to reorder experience.

Following the publication of 'East Coker', Eliot moved quickly on to 'The Dry Salvages'. The title comes from a group of rocks off Cape Ann that Eliot knew from his youth as a sailor, and it is the Massachusetts coast and the Mississippi river, the two dominant physical experiences of his childhood, that provide the setting of this poem. Eliot is one of the greatest nature poets of the twentieth century, and this quartet is a magnificent evocation of the power of a Nature too easily ignored in an industrialized society.[10] Once again the poem focuses on the immensity of the present, casting into doubt all our previous identifications and pregnant with unforeseeable futures. The theological text is neither Buddhist nor Christian but the sacred text of Hinduism, which had provided the final reference of *The Waste Land* – the *Bhagavad-Gita*. The precise reference is to the moment at which Arjuna prepares for combat against an enemy that he knows too well. Arjuna is fearful of the consequences of his actions, particularly that in the course of the battle he will kill his own kin. Krishna counsels him that we must act from our position in the present; the attempt to second guess the consequences of our actions is futile. We must act, and here the poem restates one of the themes of all three later quartets, as though every moment is the moment of our death.

'The Dry Salvages' seems the most obviously contemporary of the four poems. Krishna's advice to Arjuna could be the advice to any soldier reluctant to participate in the second instalment of Europe's civil war; and the evocation of the United States has a particular urgency at a moment when American entry into the war was absolutely vital to Britain's cause. Those who favour a strictly Christian interpretation of *Four Quartets* are bothered by the appearance of Krishna at such a crucial juncture. But it should be noted that, if Eliot maintained a frightening orthodoxy in his prose writings (the year after he finished *Four Quartets* he would devote a twenty-page pamphlet to denouncing plans for unity amongst the Christian churches of India), it is very difficult to bend *Four Quartets* into orthodox Christianity. Much as the prose writing of the immediate post-war years argues for a European tradition that the poetry calls into question, Eliot's undoubted commitment to the Creed and practice of his Church does not translate directly into his poetry. And, in European terms, there was probably an important reason to reach back to the Hindu past. There can be few more exciting moments in the history of Western thought than the evening of 2 February 1786, when Sir William Jones rose to address the Asiatic society in Calcutta. Latin and Greek had been the unquestioned moments of cultural origin since the Renaissance and the unquestioned models against which all

61

other languages had to be measured. Jones, talking of Hindu civilization, cast this fundamental assumption into doubt:

> The Sanskrit language is of a wonderful structure; more perfect than the Greek, more copious than the Latin, and more exquisitely refined than either, yet bearing to both of them a stronger affinity, both in the roots of the verbs and the forms of grammar, than could possibly have been produced by accident; so strong indeed, that no philologer could examine them all three, without believing them to have sprung from some common source.

Here in broad outline is the research programme into the interconnections of the Indo-European languages that was to occupy the universities of Europe, and pre-eminently of Germany, throughout the nineteenth century. It was this comparative philology in which Eliot had been trained at Harvard, and it is this philology that provides much of the theory of Eliot's poetry, but it was this philology too that had provided the Nazis not only with their key term of 'Aryan' but also with their key symbol, the swastika. It seems at least plausible to me that, in turning once again to the Hindu texts of his youth, Eliot was laying claim to the whole tradition that the Nazis had sought to appropriate.

'The Dry Salvages' had been finished incredibly quickly after 'East Coker', but the final poem, 'Little Gidding', was to take nearly two years and many drafts.[11] For Eliot the first problem was that all three of the previous poems were attached to specific emotions that the three places evoked in him, but the fourth place, Little Gidding, was simply an idea – the idea that the previous poems could be gathered up in a final translation into the process of history, so that the private illumination of 'Burnt Norton', the public tradition of 'East Coker' and the personal memory of 'The Dry Salvages' could be subsumed into a moment both historical and transcendental. Little Gidding was the place chosen because it served two historical purposes. The site of that most paradoxical of entities – an Anglican monastery – it was clearly a place that united the Church of England to medieval Catholicism. But, in addition, it had furnished shelter to Charles I as he fled from the final fatal battle at Naseby on his way to eventual imprisonment and death. Eliot never wavered in his opposition to the Puritans who had defeated Charles. It was they who had founded the modern state of Britain with

Cromwell's defeat of the Scots at Dundee and his massacres of the Irish at Drogheda and Wexford, it was they who had provided the ideology and the people for the colonization of America. Whether one regarded them from the economic point of view as the prophets of capitalism, from the political point of view as the first liberal democrats or from a literary perspective as those who had fatally 'dissociated sensibility', splitting feeling and thought in the scientific revolution, they constituted the enemy against which Eliot had polemicized over three decades. But at this moment in the fight against Hitler's Germany, such differences were set at naught. 'Little Gidding' guarantees the authenticity of the link between the English Church and Latin Europe; perhaps more importantly, it allows, in its third section, for a final reconciliation of the English Civil War.

The opening is vividly unreal. A winter's day in which the snow looks like spring blossom, the paradoxes of time made visible and a place that is both essential and completely unnecessary. Essential because we must always be in a particular place as we are at a particular time, unnecessary because, in fact, any place and any time are appropriate for truths that are eternal. Here Eliot is at his most Hegelian because the final paradox is that we come to our consciousness within a national culture and eternity is always glimpsed from a national perspective. The second section opens with the expected lyric, which uses the four elements to sing of death and which in turn is followed by the voice of poet, meditating as he has done in the previous poems on the very process of poetry. We have become used to a conversational tone, but what we find here is the most sophisticated call and response. Eliot has already attempted many of the metres of English verse. Now he imitates his great European master. When he wrote the *Divine Comedy*, Dante combined a three-line unit of sense with an overlapping rhyme scheme in which a new element was introduced after the third time a rhyme was used, terza rima. Terza rima is particularly difficult to imitate in English, because it depends on a language like Italian that, because of its limited number of word endings, contains a great number of rhyme words. Eliot solved this difficulty by avoiding rhyme altogether and producing a totally original metre in which Dante's three-line organization is married to the most supple of blank verse.

Dante's *Inferno* is most famous for its vistas of Hell and for the encounters of the poet with the souls who emerge out of its darkness visible. In this final poem Eliot sets such an encounter in the aftermath of a London air-raid – the air still thick with dust from the houses pulverized by German bombers. But this most industrial of landscapes is naturalized – the bomber becomes a dove with a tongue of flame – and it is in this imaginary urban landscape that the poet meets and talks over his life with a brother poet. We know from earlier drafts that the poet was originally named as Yeats, but he is both 'one and many', and one of the many is Dante himself. For the brother poet's final message is not infernal but purgatorial. From the waste of one's own life, there is a possible restoration 'by that refining fire'.

The notion of suffering for one's sins runs deep in Eliot's poetry, particularly in unpublished poems about martyrdom that he wrote as he completed his Harvard thesis. That we can be redeemed only by flame is not a popular message in a world where all appetites are potentially good and any mention of sin is a social solecism. But in this poem the fire of Purgatory is also the fire of love, and the two cannot be dissociated. After the reconciliation with the dead of both factions of English history, it is the 'unfamiliar Name' of Love that is revealed as the true source of the burning fire.

And now Eliot in the fifth section of 'Little Gidding' moves into the final celebration of a life that is both historical and individual, national and universal, when 'History is now and England'. And, in the very final passage of the poem, the river and the sea of 'The Dry Salvages' and the laughing children of 'Burnt Norton' return, but now caught in a pattern in which the refrain assures us that, in the words of the medieval mystic Dame Julian of Norwich, 'all shall be well and all manner of things shall be well'. And Eliot in his final lines makes the fire flare up into a pattern of a rose, the universal element taking on the form of the national symbol. Throughout his writing of the last three quartets, Eliot had been much aided by friends to whom he confided drafts and asked for comments. Chief amongst these, as Eliot acknowledged when he published the poems together in 1944 with the title of *Four Quartets*, was John Hayward. An accomplished editor, Hayward, who was paralysed from an early age by muscular

64

dystrophy, was to live with Eliot for the first decade after the war, but they were already close friends. There is something fitting in the fact that the final line of the poem was corrected by Hayward. Eliot had written 'and the fire and the rose are the same', but Hayward suggested that 'one' would be better than 'the same'. There can be little doubt that Hayward is right, the losing of the definite article, the gaining of the pun of 'one' and 'won', and the emphasis on the indivisibility of this union make 'one' a much more dramatic conclusion than 'same'. There is even an advantage of historical resonance. 'Same' is introduced into English at the time of the Danish invasions of the eighth and ninth centuries; 'one' is an Anglo-Saxon pronoun reaching back to the oldest layer of the language.

There are no doubt many reasons why Eliot took so long to finish 'Little Gidding', but the most obvious is that its triumphant conclusion was impossible to sustain while England faced military defeat. By the autumn of 1942, the entry of both the United States and Soviet Russia into the war made final victory probable, and Eliot completed and published his poem at almost exactly the moment that the Eighth Army's victory at El Alamein announced a clear turning of the tide.

I have in this very brief reading emphasized the historical setting of *Four Quartets*, and it does seem important to me to grasp how the fusion of the personal, the national and the universal that the poem performs makes sense in the context of 1940–2 in a way that it would not have at any other time. But I do not want to suggest that this historical reading does more than illuminate the 'ground' of the poem. What the poem actually does is to celebrate the intensity of each instant of life. In the final chapter of *Mimesis*, Erich Auerbach brings his study of representation in the West to a close with a reading of a passage from Virginia Woolf's *To the Lighthouse*. For Auerbach, the detailed description of a moment of repairing a sock that encompasses the memories and thoughts of Mrs Ramsay marks the triumphant conclusion of the Western attempt to represent reality. This, for Auerbach, is the modernist democratization of experience in which each instant is charged with the full weight of being; the narratives of history and biography laid bare as retrospective and misleading fictions. Woolf and Eliot had a close friendship, which their barbed comments about each other do not entirely hide. Their writing crossed institutionally in the Woolfs' publishing house and crossed formally in the reaction to Joyce's *Ulysses*. Much of what Auerbach says about Woolf can also be said of Eliot. *Four Quartets* participates fully in that modernist determination to overcharge language with meaning so that the text yields a fresh meaning on every reading, altering as we alter, always open to fresh interpretation. If in this respect it is quintessentially modernist, it is in one respect *sui generis*. For most of modernism, including *The Waste Land*, the road to the infinity of experience and meaning is achieved through the disruption of the unity of the speaking subject. *Four Quartets* opens both world and word, while maintaining a voice that, although it adopts different tones and registers, remains one.

4

The Definition of Culture

It may seem strange to claim Eliot for a modernism committed to the democratization of experience when he remained throughout his life attached to notions of hierarchical and class societies. But the move from the aesthetic to the political is rarely simple. It is a curiosity of Eliot's amazingly productive writing life that the only really long discursive text he wrote was his doctoral dissertation. Many books were mooted, but they always ended up as collections of essays or published lectures. My own suspicion is that Eliot never completed a book-length project because he would have had great difficulty in articulating his belief in a national language as the genuine spirit of a people other than in the elliptical and enigmatic fragments that we have scattered through his essays and poems. Had he done so it might have seemed easier to reconcile the democratic thrust of his poetry with his authoritarian and conservative politics. His very last major prose work *Notes towards the Definition of Culture* is the closest we get to a full statement of his cultural theories and it is a short book itself made up of disparate texts – some occasional (lectures he gave in Germany immediately after the war on European culture), some more clearly designed for publication as a continuous argument.

In taking aim at culture, Eliot was clearly and explicitly taking aim at the beliefs of the victors in the Second World War both international – the cultural ambitions of organizations such as UNESCO – and national – the cultural policies of the newly elected Labour government. It should be said that these beliefs are in many respects current. Culture is held to be a good that should be freely available to as many of the people as possible, and, if arguments over the content of that culture (above all questions of popular versus canonical culture) have proliferated, the basic assumption that culture is a good to be widely distributed animates much of the discourses and practices of state support of the arts in the Western world. Eliot argues that treating culture as a separable part of society is impossible: the great works of culture grow out of the culture of a whole people; traditional culture is tied to the class society that has produced it. Do away with classes and you will do away with traditional culture. You may value equality more than you do traditional culture but do not think that you can have one and retain the other. When Eliot wrote 'Tradition and the Individual Talent' he was clearing the ground for the poetry he was going to write; *Notes towards the Definition of Culture* is a defence of the audience who would read the poetry he had written.

From the late 1930s Eliot had participated in a group of Christian intellectuals who called themselves The Moot, and his short book on the idea of a Christian society that he had published just before the war had grown out of these discussions. One of the most considerable of the figures who attended the Moot was Karl Mannheim, a Hungarian-born émigré from Nazi Germany who had been formed in that same mix of Idealist philosophy and social science that had characterized Eliot's study at Harvard. Mannheim accepted that any simple equalization of society was impossible; the complexity of the differential functions of society meant that classes would have to be replaced by elites. For Eliot, however, if you divorce these elite functions from their traditional hereditary class basis, then you will no longer have the most developed forms of European culture. A culture is not transmitted through an education system, still less through systems of state sponsorship, but through a whole way of life. Destroy the developed class system of the European nations and you will destroy the culture that goes with it.

Eliot's views were, as he himself recognized, completely at odds with the dominant theories and ideologies of the time, and few took the great poet, now adorned with both the Order of Merit and the Nobel Prize, very seriously. One who did was Raymond Williams, who, writing ten years later in *Culture and Society*, rejoiced over 'such a Conservative'.[1] Indeed, Williams's study can be understood at one level as a decade-long response to Eliot's own book, taking the word culture and tracing its meanings through the nineteenth-century reaction to the new forms of industrialized society. Williams rejoiced not in Eliot's conservative conclusions but in his emphasis on culture as a 'whole way of life' and on his insistence, against Fabian liberalism, that particular forms of culture could not be separated out and transmitted independently of their complex social context. At the same time, Eliot's understanding of this 'whole way of life' in terms of an imaginary and idealized agrarian past is for Williams very limited. Above all, Eliot ignores the importance of economic activity as a determinant of the culture of a society. Eliot derives classes from the increasing differentiation of activity within a complex society. Classes thus become a natural feature of modern societies. But Eliot completely ignores the role of property in this history and its determining role in class formation. For Williams, Eliot's organic model is too simple, like that of Coleridge and Carlyle: it is essentially an imaginary and never-existing feudalism constructed as an alternative to the horrors of industrial capitalism.

But the crucial point that Eliot makes for Williams is that one cannot separate out a part of the culture – the arts – and assume that it can be reproduced without the general culture that gave it form. In *Culture and Society*, Williams took the anthropological notion of culture that Eliot had worked with all his life, and went back to the social thinking that had developed that notion for the anthropologists. Three years later, in *The Long Revolution*, Williams offered an alternative history of the nineteenth century in which the pessimistic analysis of industrial development is complemented by a history of communication from the postal service to newspapers to television. The backdrop to this history is the development of universal education, and the belief is that these new technologies of communication (to which we now have to add the digital revolution) allow the possibility of an ever-greater democratic conversation in which the experiences of each will contribute to the understanding of all. If the capitalist forms that have developed and currently control these means of communication hold back their human potential, the long revolution of education and the evolution of the economic forms themselves promise a different future. It may seem difficult to sustain such a faith when, to take merely one example, the latest developments in cable television are crucial both to the growth of fundamentalist Christianity and to a willed global insensitivity in the United States. But, if there is to be any global hope, it must depend on just such a long revolution.

In a long historical perspective, this revolution may be most significant in terms of a fundamental change in the status of the written word. The seventeenth century accomplished an identification of the printed word with the language that was to last three centuries. Eliot was born into a world in which this identification was the most certain of evidences. He died in a world where film, television, recorded music and radio had displaced that identification forever. For Eliot this was clear evidence of a decline in standards; for us it means that the question of the place of our literary heritage in the general culture is an open one. Eliot in his pessimism foresaw a moment when there would be 'no culture', and in one sense this pessimism has come to pass. If we think of those friends to whom he distributed drafts of his final poems, then there are probably no readers left for *Four Quartets*, no cohort of Oxbridge graduates deeply versed in the culture of cultural antiquity, in Christian theology and in English history and letters. But there are potentially many more readers; it is doubtful whether Eliot could ever have considered the number of students now reading for English as a university degree. If no students, or indeed teachers, now inhabit the intellectual world that produced *Four Quartets'* first readership, there are extraordinary resources of reference and scholarship that make the poems much more widely available than when they were first published. And, indeed, one of the virtues of studying Eliot's poetry is that it provides one of the most direct forms of access to that European Latin culture that Eliot so revered and that has all but disappeared, along with the teaching of classics in the school.

But, if we still wish to teach Eliot, this useful feature of his work cannot be the final justification. That justification must come in the hopes of a much richer and a much more complicated culture than one based on the supremacy of the written word. Williams in *The Long Revolution* held out the promise of such a culture and most importantly no longer considered it within the political perspective of a single generation. This shift of temporal focus also allowed Williams to avoid that mistake of all cultural commentators from Arnold and Nietzsche on: an overweening importance for the role of the cultural critic. One of the great virtues of *Culture and Society* and *The Long Revolution* is that they award no particular importance to the work of the critic. Such efforts will feed into new formulations and understandings, but they have no way of specifying in advance the crucial developments within the long and complex revolution.

Williams, at all stages of his career, was sure that it was obscene that the canon of English literature should be used to justify a particular social class. However, he never made the mistake of identifying the canon with the exclusions it was used to operate. The question of the place of the canon of English literature within the new world of the mass culture of the twentieth and twenty-first centuries should be one of the most vivid of contemporary debates. However, the development of the study of film and television has not, in the universities, stimulated such discussion. If you watch the films of Chris Marker or Terence Davies, you could argue that Eliot has had more influence on film-makers than he has had on poets, but such an argument does not easily find a place in either the university or the film school. Amongst those who teach traditional literature, there is now an influential position that merely identifies traditional aesthetic taste with a class position of exploitation. While it is possible to understand this argument in historical terms as a reaction to a mannered aesthetic snobbery, it seems a genuine waste that those who are best placed to articulate the complexity of traditional culture are content merely to simplify it.

When you put together a belief in the cultural centrality of the critic with a fixation on literature as class oppression, you get the situation, tragic or ludicrous according to taste, in which many teachers of English literature seem to think that their job is to unmask the ideological pretensions of the literature they are teaching. While such readings never address either the intentions of the writers or the desires of contemporary readers, they do nourish a sense of social importance. But it is just this sense of importance that has to be abandoned if one is to do justice to the complexity both of the literary tradition and of the current cultural situation. Eliot states many times in *Notes towards the Definition of Culture* that culture is impossible without

71

a religious foundation. No argument is made for this assertion, and it is difficult to know exactly what he means by it. But it may be as simple as saying that a culture must have a relation to a time longer than history and a purpose greater than any single generation. In this sense, Auerbach and Williams, both writing as heirs of their nineteenth-century traditions, find a common belief in an ideology that links progress in democracy to complexity of communication. This ideology has been mocked and derided in recent decades both theoretically in terms of all the anti-Hegelianisms of French structuralism and politically because of its continuous abuse by Western politicians. However, it should be noted that Williams's biologically rooted Hegelianism does not fall prey to many of the anti-Hegelian arguments, because it is sceptical about any attempt to grasp the moment of totalization. Indeed, one might argue that even to apply the term Hegelian to Williams, Auerbach and Eliot is already too specific. What these authors share is an abiding belief in the reality of those communicative patterns that make our being deeply historical.

It is certain that a deeper understanding of those patterns is going to have to include consideration of sexual and racial difference, which must complicate this ideology of European progress, not least when it fully reckons the history of the non-European. But it is within this perspective that one can best envisage the future value of Eliot's work. The use of language as sound, the weaving of melodies out of the spoken word, is just as central to the art of Tupac Shakur or Eminem as it is to Eliot. However, the cultural tradition in which Eliot places himself, the arc of history that he seeks to complete, produces a very specific complexity. It is this complexity and its centrality to notions of civilization that remain fully contemporary. Benjamin famously commented that there were no monuments of civilization that were not also monuments to barbarism, but he did not mean by this that we should abandon the struggle for civilization. If Eliot and the canon of English poetry will not be central to this future civilization, one reason may be that it will have no centres. But it is difficult to imagine a civilized future in which they will have no place.

The long revolution provides a Utopian limit for our cultural questions, but it does not provide immediate justifications. The contemporary paradoxes of information beggar the imagination. Never has so much been known by so many to so little purpose. The decision of the United States and England to go to war in Iraq to destroy arms that did not exist can serve as merely one example of our total inability to link the ability to collect information to the decision-making processes in our society.[2] We may make it an article of faith that eventually we will overcome this inability, but nothing suggests that this over-coming is for our, or indeed for our children's, lifetime. In these circumstances, a Utopian politics needs to be supplemented by a Stoic ethics. If one can believe in the future value of Eliot's work, the reason for teaching it in the present must simply be in terms of our own belief in its quality, the pleasure and instruction that it has provided to us and that we, in turn, attempt to provide to our students.

How to balance the Utopian future and the Stoic present cannot be the work of one person or one moment; all that individually we can say is that we have found these texts of value and hope that others will also find them valuable. But it is crucial that we do not also suggest that valuing them makes us valuable; for that, indeed, is how literature and its transmission have been used to breed contempt. And, if we are sure in our determination to value Eliot's poetry, this means that we are also sure that its value will always be in question.

In recent years much debate on Eliot has turned on his anti-Semitism. Anthony Julius's 1995 book reopened a debate that dated from 1933 when in lectures at Virginia University entitled 'After Strange Gods' Eliot stated that 'reasons of race and religion combine to make any large number of free thinking Jews undesirable' (*ASG* 20). Eliot claimed to be sick at the time[3] (the lectures were given as he was separating from his wife), and he always refused to republish them, but this direct statement of anti-Semitism in the year that Hitler came to power delivered in a segregationist setting remains a significant element in any final assessment of Eliot. Julius's book does two things. First, it argues beyond doubt that the anti-Semitic poems of the earlier *Ara Vos Prec* period were deeply, thoroughly, even poetically, if poetry is to do with condensation and intensification of meaning, anti-Semitic. Their anti-Semitism was not of the surface but of the depths, gathering together into half lines decades of European politics and centuries of Christian lies. There is no doubt that Julius's readings compel assent and that we must give an account of Eliot's intellectual and poetic development which acknowledges this. The anti-Semitism of *Ara Vos Prec* arrives between the confidence in the 'European Mind' of 'Tradition and the Individual Talent' and the discovery of Joyce's 'mythical method' of *The Waste Land*. It is undoubtedly the most desperate of Eliot's strategies to guarantee the legacy of European civilization and is adopted at what may have been the most tortured time in his marriage. Nonetheless, it is a strategy that is explored in depth and may call into question the very European heritage itself; it is certain that Eliot himself came to feel that the only unquestioned guarantor of this heritage was Christianity.

If the centrality of this moment of anti-Semitism is admitted, the question then becomes how we value the poems of that period. 'Gerontion' remains for me one of the great poems – its anti-Semitism part of the collapse of Europe that the poem dramatizes and predicts. The other poems are much more problematic, but they are problematic not simply because their anti-Semitism is more viscerally unpleasant but because the unity of European civilization that the Jews pollute is always a fake unity. To pursue this line of thought is to realize that the anti-Semitism is merely one aspect of a racist conception of Europe. The passage about Jews in 'After Strange Gods' comes within one of the most direct statements of why Eliot feels it impossible to give his allegiance to the Yankee victors in the Civil War – his hopes lie with the South: 'Yet I think the chances for the re-establishment of a native culture are perhaps better here than in New England. You are further away from New York; you have been less industrialized and less invaded by foreign races; and you have a more opulent soil' (*ASG* 16–17). This statement makes clear that Eliot's statements about Jews is part of a wider distaste for 'foreign races', and we have seen this already in the poems. That distaste is itself in part a product of a highly nationalist theory of culture, a determination to identify a people and a language that form an organic whole. It is this theory that leads him from America to England and from Unitarianism to Anglo-Catholicism. It is this theory that underpins the *Four Quartets*, in which English culture has no Celtic margins. It is this theory that allows a reading of Dante as the poet of European culture without considering the Florentine's debts to the Arab culture of Spain. Both Dante's great theoretical master, Aquinas, and his poetic models from the *langue d'oc* found their textual origins in the society of Moorish Spain. Most importantly, perhaps, there is a complete erasure of Africa from the history of Europe. Bololand may have been abandoned, but there is no engagement with the triangle of trade that linked Europe, the Southern United States and Africa from the seventeenth century on. The 'dead negroes' on the Mississippi in 'The Dry Salvages' is the only African contribution to Eliot's vision of the United States. *The Cocktail Party*'s account of monkey-eating cannibals in Kinkanja is a saloon-bar account of Africa. It is only if Eliot's cultural theory is understood within this wider context that we can engage with it properly, either dissociating it from the poetry or attempting to find within its notions of order and unity elements that we can still value.

The anti-Hegelianism of the structuralist revolution had many components, but perhaps the most important was the total rejection both of those right-wing versions of Hegelianism (Hegel, Kojeve, more recently Fukuyama) that found history's apotheosis in the current political dispensation or those left-wing versions that announced its culmination in the industrial proletariat's coming revolution. Against a history whose outcome was always known in advance, the anti-Hegelians stressed the complexities of human meaning. Whether it was Foucault sketching the way that a variety of heterogeneous factors produced the practice of clinical medicine, Barthes analysing the poetics of wrestling, Althusser emphasizing the different discourses of Marx's early texts or Lévi-Strauss insisting on the elaborate structure of mythological narrative, all the structuralists, whether they accepted the name or not, insisted on a precise attention to the specificities of given discourses. They would not be gathered up in some totalizing narrative whose happy end was either the most self-satisfied bourgeois citizen or his almost-as-satisfied petit bourgeois brother – the revolutionary militant.

This work was, itself, an after effect of the modernism of the early 1920s, a working-out in intellectual terms of the attention to language that had already stripped bare the certainties of self and meaning that had underpinned the notion of the Western hero. Instead of that hero we were offered the subversive, the transgressive, the hybrid, not a moment of totalization but the moment of negativity. No European literary figure articulated this negativity more thoroughly than Joyce after *Ulysses*, his seventeen years of *Work in Progress* supported throughout and finally published as *Finnegans Wake* in 1939 by Eliot's Faber & Faber. There can be no doubt that Eliot held Joyce in the highest regard: the terms of the praise both in the famous review of *Ulysses* and in 'After Strange Gods' are quite different from the praise for any other contemporary. However, it is less often remarked that Eliot seems to have been one of the very few of his contemporaries that Joyce read with care and attention. There is considerable evidence that Joyce was impressed by *The Waste Land*.[4] He constantly complained of its thefts from *Ulysses*, but the most fundamental music of *Finnegans Wake*, the sound of a female voice breaking through a male one, is first heard most clearly in the opening lines of *The Waste Land*.

In many ways *Finnegans Wake* and *Four Quartets* perform a necessary complementarity. Eliot came from a people used to rule, a people who had chosen their religion and their fate, a people unbeaten in significant battle; Joyce from a people who had known persecutions so violent, famines so terrible, defeats so total that they had abandoned their very language. Eliot could not abandon his patrimony and his works all shore fragments against ruins, rescuing Europe from European history. But, for an Irishman, European history ends with the Dark Ages, as, from the twelfth century on, the history of Ireland and Europe is the history of English colonialism. Joyce has to go back to the Dark Ages before he can recognize a European identity that includes an Irish one. For Joyce, Europe is the moment before the German tribes fashion nations out of the ruins of the Roman Empire. Here there is no purity of races or languages but merely 'miscegenations on miscegenations'. *Finnegans Wake* is a desperate attempt to provide a model of liberation not tied to the political or psychological forms of the oppressor. The aim is to provide a song of the great hero Finn, the Norse invader, to the tune of Tim Finnegan, the drunken emigrant bricklayer. Eliot and Joyce both write in a moment that sees the end of the unquestioned dominance of the literary

76

language in the culture and a fundamental reconfiguration of our experience of sexuality.

Four Quartets weaves from the metres of English poetry a final form of English identity. Eliot in the *Quartets* constructs a pattern of existence forged in the sublimation of sexuality and an abandonment of popular culture. *Finnegans Wake* ends with one of the most moving passages in English literature when Anna Livia flows down to her sea of death. In Joyce death and sexuality are one: the moment of death as the salt sea washes into the fresh water is also the moment of sexual recognition of the father. Joyce's monologue is the most moving determination to claim the joy of existence from a river of sorrow, a hymn of acceptance of pain as both Europe and his own family crash towards destruction; *Four Quartets* ends with a woman's voice breaking through a male monologue to assure us that 'all shall be well and all manner of things shall be well'. The voice is that of Dame Julian of Norwich, the voice of a woman withdrawn from the world and from sexuality. It is that voice that brings to a conclusion Eliot's prayer of thanks for deliverance in battle. And it is in the form of that prayer that Eliot fashions a deliverance from his anguished earlier self. In the early poems the only option to disgusting and deadly sexuality was the fixed and fixated self of 'Rhapsody on a Windy Night'. But Eliot has now undertaken a talking cure with God, and found in prayer the possibility of giving misery an apparent meaning, a discipline of language that disintegrated the self only to reform it in union with God. The renunciation of sexuality is what allows Eliot access to the dance at the still point of the turning world.

The renunciation of sexuality has not enjoyed a great press in the last fifty years. As sex has become one of the key elements in consumer culture, to renounce one's sexuality is as great a social sin as to stop spending. But as paedophilia goes epidemic and child porn and sex tourism prove ever-growing markets, it may be that sublimation will come to seem as crucial as transgression. Indeed, when transgression is no longer possible, when there are no limits at which we can experience the forbidden, then sublimation may become the very condition of desire.

It is impossible to second guess the future. The configurations of sex, religion and art in the era of mass communication surprise daily. The settlement inaugurated by the capitalist mode of production, the settlement of the Reformation, of English as a national language, of the model of civilized manhood, dissolves daily. Eliot and Joyce both inherit and undo this settlement in all its neo-classical, Romantic and Victorian forms. They can have no literary successors for the moment of literary modernism; the moment at which an art becomes aware of its history as a medium is unrepeatable. Both Eliot and Joyce press at the very limits of the existing form of the literary, as they both envisage multimedia forms that the technology of the time could not provide. It is not foolish to hope that the lessons they teach and the pleasures they fashion reach into the new forms of culture. These new forms are global in industrial production and iconic in their forms of representation; their links with the national cultures tied to the symbolic representation of writing are the stuff of the world's future.

The book no longer enjoys the unquestioned supremacy inaugurated by Johannes Gutenberg's publication of his Bible on movable type in 1455. Chronologically that dominance lasted 440 years. In 1895 the Lumière Brothers invented the cinema with their projection of images to paying customers. Joyce and Woolf were 13, Eliot 8. In one year the invention had gone global. The same decade saw the beginning of the mass production of gramophones. But, despite the extraordinary interaction of music, image and writing that constitutes contemporary culture, our education systems at every level from primary to graduate school separate the teaching of these different media. In no education system that I am aware of is the teaching of traditional literacy linked to an investigation of our new technological forms. In no university or film school is the production of new media linked to an appreciation of the greatest literature. It is possible to regard modernism as a dead end, the moment at which the idea of the artist broke against the reality of a democratic public. But it is also possible to see modernism as a beginning, as the start of a long revolution that will not be finished until every existence is illuminated.

5

Happiness and Poetry

Four Quartets held out the ideal of a life open to the most radical revision in the midst of the most habitual of existences. In late 1957, at the age of 68, Eliot proposed to his 30-year-old secretary Valerie Fletcher, and she accepted. His last years seem to have been as happy as the majority of his life had been full of woe. He told a reporter from the *Daily Express*: 'I am thinking of taking up dancing lessons again as I have not danced at all for some years.' The story goes that when he left his flat the day before he was to get married, he gave his flat mate of more than a decade, John Hayward, a letter with the request that he open it on the morrow. Hayward said that was nonsense and read the letter, which informed him of the marriage, with Eliot standing in front of him. I suppose this is 'lurve', he said, producing the word in its full vulgarity. 'Yes I suppose it is,' replied Eliot.[1] When young, he had been a man so crippled by social and sexual anxieties that he could not imagine himself shaving in front of a woman; in his last years he was content to let his young wife shave him. He died with her name on his lips.

There can be little doubt that he foresaw with loathing the avalanche of interest surrounding his life. No biography, he said as early as 1925; 'suppress everything suppressible,' he instructed Hayward when he was his literary executor. When in 1952 a young academic, John Peters, published a reading of *The Waste Land* as centred in an experience of homosexual love, Eliot, through legal and moral threats had every copy of the magazine destroyed. Some have read this as a panicked reaction to an unwelcome revelation about homosexuality. It is as easy to understand it as a worldly wise Eliot making sure that no one discussed his early marriage. But, while it is difficult not to sympathize with anyone who does not want his life monstered by what Joyce called the biografiends, it is difficult to regret the knowledge of recent years. Much of it adds a further level of meaning and reference to the texts and makes them considerably richer. We can accept much of Eliot's theory of impersonality, the belief that experience should be stripped of its narcissistic carapace, similar to Barthes's call for the death of the author, and still hold that the poetry is a product of a life. But the information should be used to complicate not to simplify the poetry.

In fact most of the recent discussion of Eliot reduces the complexity of a life to the stereotype of the chat show. It is clear that the marriage with Vivien was Hell. But what do we mean by Hell when it produces the poetry of *The Waste Land* and the first burst of *The Criterion*? It is true we know things to Eliot's discredit. He had a very violent temper at times. But easily the most scathing picture of this grumpy old man is provided by Eliot himself:

> The tiger in the tiger-pit
> Is not more irritable than I.
> The whipping tail is not more still
> Than when I smell the enemy
> Writhing in the essential blood
> Or dangling from the friendly tree.

Perhaps the outburst of temper that makes the most painful reading was his fury when his sister-in-law introduced Emily Hale into the company when Eliot, newly widowed, knew that his dream of marrying Emily was just that.[2] But he then went to tell Emily the truth, and, if he broke her heart, who would hold him culpable?

The truth is that most of the matters on which people pronounce with great moral certainty are so complicated that they defy any easy judgement. Of all the charges made against Eliot, perhaps the most serious is his refusal to see Vivien after he had separated from her in 1933. Vivien refused to accept this separation and spent the next years wandering around London vainly trying to effect a reconciliation. It is easy to castigate Eliot for his inability to make the minimal gesture of meeting his former wife. But so to do is to ignore the fact that Eliot and Vivien had lived a *folie à deux* for a decade, and Eliot may well have feared that he would be plunged back into that madness if he encountered her. And, indeed, the madness that he feared may have been more than personal. When in November 1935 Vivien finally did track him down to a public reading, she was wearing her Fascist uniform. It may well have been that a reconciliation with Vivien would also have entailed a fall into the Fascism she had embraced so enthusiastically. When we consider the range of Eliot's abilities, we should perhaps be grateful that Mosely's Fascists did not employ his talents – writing speeches for the leader, songs for the troops and slogans for the campaign. This is, of course, supposition, but it is merely meant to indicate how foolish it is to reach judgements about matters so complicated.

As a student in the late 1960s I found Eliot's politics intolerable, while never failing to be moved by the poetry. 'For us, there is only the trying. The rest is not our business' seemed a recipe for conservative quietism. A generation on, it is easy to recognize that it is the height of egocentric foolishness, a wilful disregard of all our historical and biological knowledge, to think that the most important social transformations can be accomplished in a lifetime. But there is an eagerness to be defeated in social battle in Eliot's lines that still jars. There is a prim distaste for the great unwashed that occasionally mars both prose and poetry, and of which the anti-Semitism is merely one symptom.

But he remains one of the greatest poets in the English language. He brought more knowledge to this task than even Milton or Pope. He had read widely in the literature and thought of modern Europe and classical antiquity. He had enjoyed a philosophical training that encompassed the tradition of German Idealism as well as the very beginnings of analytic philosophy. And in that period he had also studied Sanscrit and its scriptures. Above all he read English poetry with an attention that still rewards. His knowledge of business was also remarkable, Lloyds, *The Criterion*, Faber & Faber – you have to go back to Shakespeare or Richardson before you find a major writer with such extensive business interests.

Horace says that it takes a hundred years to secure a work's reputation. *The Waste Land* has eighteen years to go, *Four Quartets* a full forty, 'Prufrock' just six. It is difficult to think that Eliot will not figure in any anthology of English poetry for as long as we

81

can imagine, but will he find a mention in the literary and cultural dictionaries in Mandarin, Hindi and Swahili of 3,000 A.D.? He might. There have been few who have thought more of the judgement of eternity on poetry; in the end he was content that he judged *The Waste Land* and the last three of the *Four Quartets* good. The art he practised is as old as speech and writing. It needs no instrument to accompany it, no setting to make it live. It is there in the first sounds that are exchanged with the mother; it accompanies us in the last words over our grave. We go to writing for many things, for information, for identification, for stories. But great poetry takes us to language itself, to the medium in which our being takes form, and it allows us to meditate on the form of our being. Eliot is one of the great poets of time, of the paradox that every instant is infinite and yet caught in a linear series. He enjoyed great worldly success from very early, but the poetry reveals a young man so crippled by the need for self-possession that it is only the overheard moments of a mechanical street piano that can bring any music to his world. But it is such moments that he is determined to pursue, and his poetry is that pursuit:

> For most of us, there is only the unattended
> Moment, the moment in and out of time,
> The distraction fit, lost in a shaft of sunlight,
> The wild thyme unseen, or the winter lightning
> Or the waterfall, or music heard so deeply
> That it is not heard at all, but you are the music
> While the music lasts.

Notes

INTRODUCTION

1. Both Vivien and Vivenne were used.
2. 'in its sources, in its emotional springs, it comes from America' *Paris Review*, 21 Spring/Summer 1959, 70.

CHAPTER 1. EARLY LIFE

1. Henri Bergson, *Matter and Memory* (New York: Zone Books, 1988), 198.
2. Lyndall Gordon, *T. S. Eliot: An Imperfect Life* (New York: Norton, 1999), 39.
3. Sigmund Freud, *The Complete Psychological Works* (London: Hogarth Press, 1953–74), xi. 184.

CHAPTER 2. FROM HARVARD PHILOSOPHY TO LITERARY LONDON

1. See Bruce Kuklick, *The Rise of American Philosophy: Cambridge, Massachusetts, 1860–1930* (New Haven and London: Yale University Press, 1977).
2. Ibid. 290
3. *The Egoist*, 5/1 (Jan. 1918).
4. None of the existing biographies relates Eliot's reaction to Sweeney's arrival in the White House in the person of John Fitzgerald Kennedy.
5. Ezra Pound to Harriet Monroe, 30 Sept. 1914, in Ezra Pound, *Letters of Ezra Pound*, ed. D. D. Paige (London: Faber & Faber, 1951).
6. Ray Monk, *Bertrand Russell* (London: Vintage, 1997), 353–4.
7. Leonard Woolf, *Beginning Again: An Autobiography of the Years 1911–1918* (London: Hogarth Press, 1964), 34–5.

8. Monk, *Bertrand Russell*, 433–4. Russell was to befriend the Eliots, and they were to live together at various times between 1915 and 1918. For at least part of this time Russell was carrying on an affair with Vivien. This affair forms much of the subject matter of the play *Tom and Viv* and the subsequent film. The film can be very useful in the classroom, largely because of the performances of Willem Dafoe as Tom and Miranda Richardson as Viv, Dafoe studiedly deliberate, Richardson spiritedly unbalanced. But great care must be taken in showing the film to students. That Russell, that most quintessential of Cambridge figures, is academically attached to Oxford may be put down to 'dramatic licence'. But that Eliot's marriage is portrayed as social climbing is completely to misunderstand the psychosexual allure of the 'vulgar' Vivien. And the final parts of the film are a hideous attempt to simplify and apportion blame. In particular there is a dramatic device in the play that has the actor who plays Eliot appearing at the conclusion of the action as the doctor who pronounces all Viv's problems to be 'hormonal imbalances'. By using a different actor for this role, the film transforms an interesting irony into comforting claptrap.

9. Lyndall Gordon, *T. S. Eliot: An Imperfect Life* (New York: Norton, 1999), 118.

10. Carol Seymour-Jones, *Painted Shadow: A Life of Vivienne Eliot* (London: Constable, 2001), 249.

11. Peter Ackroyd, *T. S. Eliot: A Life* (London: Hamish Hamilton, 1984), 92.

12. In the notes to *Ara Vos Prec* in his Eliot bibliography, Donald Gallup writes: 'The error "Vus" for "Vos" in the title was discovered after all the sheets had been printed and was corrected only on the label. Concerning the title, Mr Eliot wrote me on 21 February 1936: "The correct title of the book is *Ara Vos Prec*. It only happened to be *Vus* on the title page because I don't know Provençal, and I was quoting from an Italian edition of Dante the editor of which apparently did not know Provençal either. It would seem that there is no such word as *Vus* in that language"' Gallup, *T. S. Eliot: A Bibliography* (London: Faber & Faber, 1969), 24.

13. B. C. Southam, *A Student's Guide to the Selected Poems of T. S.* Eliot, 6th edn. (London: Faber & Faber, 1994), 70.

14. J. M. Keynes, *The Economic Consequences of the Peace* (New York: Harcourt Brace & Howe, 1920), 5.

15. Piers Gray, *T. S. Eliot's Intellectual and Poetic Development, 1909–1922* (Brighton: Harvester, 1982), 211–13.

16. Keynes, *The Economic Consequences of the Peace*, 32. See also Tom Paulin, 'Many cunning passages' *Times Literary Supplement* (Nov. 29, 2002), 14–15.

17. Ezra Pound, *The Spirit of Romance*, rev. edn. (Norfolk, Conn., J. Laughlin, 1952), 8.
18. Quoted in Anthony Julius, *T.S. Eliot, Anti-Semitism and Literary Form*, 2nd edn. (London: Thames & Hudson, 2003), 108.
19. Gray, *T. S. Eliot's Intellectual and Poetic Development, 1909–1922*, 204.
20. To give one example, as the house agent's clerk reaches the bottom of the stairs Eliot originally had him 'at the corner where the stable is | Delays only to urinate and spit'. Pound, scratching out the lines, wisely remarked 'probably over the mark' (*WL* 47).
21. *Paris Review*, 21 (Spring/Summer 1959), 19.

CHAPTER 3. A DANCER TO GOD

1. *Eliot in a Four Piece Suit* is an aperçu of Virginia Woolf. See Lyndall Gordon *T. S. Eliot. An Imperfect Life* (London: Vintage 1998) 142.
2. Piers Gray, *T. S. Eliot's Intellectual and Poetic Development, 1909–1922* (Brighton: Harvester Press, 1982), 231.
3. Peter Ackroyd, *T. S. Eliot: A Life* (London: Hamish Hamilton, 1984), 147.
4. Ibid. 146.
5. See Colin MacCabe, *Godard: A Portrait of the Artist at 70* (London: Bloomsbury, 2003), 295. For a brilliant and thorough analysis of the importance of cinema for Eliot's poetry, see David Trotter, *Cinema and Modernism* (Oxford: Blackwell, forthcoming).
6. B. C. Southam, *A Student's Guide to the Selected Poems of T. S. Eliot*, 6th edn. (London: Faber & Faber, 1994), 221.
7. *The Criterion*, 18/71 (Jan. 1939), 271.
8. Helen Gardner, *The Art of T. S. Eliot*, preface to the sixth impression (London: Faber & Faber, 1968).
9. Auden's *Spain*, published in 1937, used a continuous refrain of 'Today the Struggle'.
10. In the *Idea of a Christian Society*, which Eliot had published just before the outbreak of war, his critique of capitalism is notable for its prescience about the long-term ecological damage wrought by industrialization: 'We are being made aware that the organization of society on the principle of private profit, as well as public destruction, is leading both to the deformation of humanity by unregulated industrialism, and to the exhaustion of natural resources, and that a good deal of our material progress is a progress for which succeeding generations may have to pay dearly' (*ICS* 61–2).
11. See Helen Gardner, *The Composition of 'Four Quartets'* (Oxford: Oxford University Press, 1978).

CHAPTER 4. THE DEFINITION OF CULTURE

1. Raymond Williams is quoting Mill on Coleridge: Williams, *Culture and Society, 1780–1950* (New York: Columbia University Press, 1983), 227.
2. It should be noted that the informational scandal of the second Iraq war is not the non-existence of weapons of mass destruction, for many believed that they existed. What is really scandalous is that Bush and Blair could go to war believing that the Iraqis would welcome democracy and freedom when these terms had been emptied of all historical or social content and certainly involved no control of their economic future.
3. T. S. Matthews, *Great Tom: Notes towards the Definition of T. S. Eliot* (New York: Harper & Row, 1974), 131.
4. Richard Ellmann, *James Joyce*, 2nd edn. (Oxford: Oxford University Press, 1983), 495.

CHAPTER 5. HAPPINESS AND POETRY

1. This story was told me by Peter Avery, Fellow of King's College, Cambridge, who had heard it from two friends of Hayward's. Accounts of Eliot's leaving the flat are contradictory. In this version Eliot considered moving in with Valerie, but Hayward would have none of it.
2. For more details, see Carol Seymour-Jones, *Painted Shadow: A Life of Vivienne Eliot* (London: Constable, 2001), 571–572.

Select Bibliography

T. S. Eliot is one of the most written-about poets and critics of the twentieth century. There is, however, no complete edition of his works, nor any biography composed with all the relevant papers available, and the only volume of his letters published ends in 1922.

MAJOR WORKS BY T. S. ELIOT

Prufrock and Other Observations (London: The Egoist, 1917).

Ezra Pound, His Metric and Poetry (New York: A. A. Knopf, 1918).

Poems (London: Hogarth Press, 1919).

'Reflections on Contemporary Poetry', *The Egoist* (July 1919).

Ara Vos Prec (London: The Ovid Press, 1920).

Poems (New York: Alfred A. Knopf, 1920).

The Sacred Wood. Essays on Poetry and Criticism (London: Methuen, 1920).

The Waste Land (New York: Boni & Liveright, 1922).

The Waste Land: A Facsimile and Transcript of the Original Drafts Including the Annotations of Ezra Pound, ed. with an intro. by Valerie Eliot (London: Faber & Faber, 1971).

Homage to John Dryden. Three Essays on Poetry of the Seventeenth Century (London: L. & V. Woolf, 1924).

Poems, 1909–1925 (London: Faber & Faber, 1925).

For Lancelot Andrewes (Garden City, NY: Doubleday, Doran & Co. Inc., 1928).

Dante (London: Faber & Faber, 1929).

Ash Wednesday (London: Faber & Faber, 1930).

Anabasis; a Poem by St-J Perse. With a Translation into English by T. S. Eliot (London: Faber & Faber, 1930).

Thoughts after Lambeth (London: Faber & Faber, 1931).

Triumphal March (London: Faber & Faber, 1931).

Selected Essays (London: Faber & Faber, 1932).

John Dryden. The Poet, the Dramatist, the Critic. Three Essays (New York: T. & E. Holliday, 1932).

Sweeney Agonistes: Fragments of an Aristophanic Melodrama (London: Faber & Faber, 1932).

The Use of Poetry and the Use of Criticism: Studies in the Relation of Criticism to Poetry in England (London: Faber & Faber, 1933).

After Strange Gods: a Primer of Modern Heresy (London: Faber & Faber, 1934).

The Rock (London: Faber & Faber, 1934).

Elizabethan Essays (London: Faber & Faber, 1934).

Murder in the Cathedral (London: Faber & Faber, 1936).

Essays Ancient and Modern (London: Faber & Faber, 1936).

Collected Poems, 1909–1935 (New York, Harcourt, Brace & Co., 1936).

The Family Reunion (London: Faber & Faber, 1939).

Old Possum's Book of Practical Cats (London: Faber & Faber, 1940).

The Idea of a Christian Society (London: Faber & Faber, 1939).

East Coker (London: Faber & Faber, 1940).

Burnt Norton (London: Faber & Faber, 1941).

The Dry Salvages (London: Faber & Faber, 1941).

Little Gidding (London: Faber & Faber, 1942).

Reunion by Destruction. Reflections on a Scheme for Church Union in South India, etc. (Westminster: Pax House, 1943).

Four Quartets (London: Faber & Faber, 1944).

Notes towards the Definition of Culture (London: Faber & Faber, 1948).

The Cocktail Party (London: Faber & Faber, 1950).

Complete Poems and Plays (New York: Harcourt, Brace, 1952).

The Confidential Clerk (London: Faber & Faber, 1954).

On Poetry and Poets (London: Faber & Faber, 1957).

The Elder Statesman (London: Faber & Faber, 1959).

Collected Plays. Murder in the Cathedral. The Family Reunion. The Cocktail Party. The Confidential Clerk. The Elder Statesman (London: Faber & Faber, 1962).

George Herbert (London: Published for the British Council and the National Book League by Longmans, Green & Co., 1962).

Collected Poems. 1909–1962 (London: Faber & Faber, 1963).

Knowledge and Experience in the Philosophy of F. H. Bradley (London: Faber & Faber 1964).

To Criticize the Critic and Other Writings (London: Faber & Faber, 1965).

Poems Written in Early Youth (London: Faber & Faber, 1967).

The Criterion, 20 Vols, October 1922–January 1939 (London: Faber & Faber 1967).

Selected Prose of T. S. Eliot, ed. Frank Kermode (London: Faber & Faber, 1975).

The Letters of T. S. Eliot, ed. Valerie Eliot (San Diego: Harcourt Brace

Jovanovich, 1988).
Inventions of the March Hare: Poems 1909–1917, ed. Christopher Ricks (London: Faber & Faber, 1996).

BIBLIOGRAPHY

Ackroyd, Peter, *T. S. Eliot* (London: Hamilton, 1984).
Brooker, Jew Spears, 'Eliot Studies: A Review and a Select Booklist', in *The Cambrige Companion to T. S. Eliot*, ed. A. David Moody (Cambridge: Cambridge University Press, 1979).
Gallup, Donald, *T. S. Eliot: A Bibliography* (London: Faber & Faber, 1969).
Martin, Mildred, *A Half-Century of Eliot Criticism; An Annotated Bibliography of Books and Articles in English 1916–1965* (Lewisberg, PA: Bucknell University Press, 1972).
Ricks, Beatrice, *T. S. Eliot: A Bibliography of Secondary Works* (Metuchen, NJ: Scarecrow Press, 1980).

CRITICISM

Ackroyd, Peter, *T. S. Eliot* (London: Hamilton, 1984).
Behr, Caroline, *T. S. Eliot: A Chronology of his Life and Works* (London: Macmillan, 1983).
Braybrooke, Neville (ed.), *T. S. Eliot: A Symposium for his Seventieth Birthday* (London: Hart-Davis, 1958).
Bush, Ronald, *T. S. Eliot: A Study in Character and Style* (Oxford: Oxford University Press, 1983).
Chiari, Joseph, *T. S. Eliot: A Memoir* (London: Enitharman, 1982).
Cooper, John Xiros, *T. S. Eliot and the Ideology of Four Quartets* (Cambridge: Cambridge University Press, 1995).
Cox, C. B., and Hinchcliffe, A. P. (eds.). *T. S. Eliot. The Wasteland. A Casebook* (London: Macmillan, 1968).
The Egoist, 5/1 (Jan. 1918).
Frye, Northrop, *T. S. Eliot* (Edinburgh & London: Oliver & Boyd, 1963).
Gardner, Helen, *The Art of T. S. Eliot* (London: Faber & Faber, 1949; sixth impression, 1968).
——— *The Composition of 'Four Quartets'* (Oxford: Oxford University Press, 1978).
Gordon, Lyndall, *T. S. Eliot: An Imperfect Life* (New York: Norton, 1999).
Grant, Michael (ed.), *T. S. Eliot: The Critical Heritage* (London: Routledge & Kegan Paul, 1982).
Gray, Piers, *T. S. Eliot's Intellectual and Poetic Development, 1909–1922* (Brighton Sussex: Harvester Press; Atlantic Highlands, N.J.:

Humanities Press, 1982).

Greene, E. J. H., *T. S. Eliot et La France* (Paris: Boivin, 1951).

Julius, Anthony, *T. S. Eliot, Anti-Semitism and Literary Form*, Rev. edn. (London: Thames & Hudson, 2003).

Kenner, Hugh. *The Invisible Poet: T. S. Eliot* (London: W. H. Allen, 1960).

Levy, William Turner, and Scherle, Victor Albert, *Affectionately, T. S. Eliot, The Story of a Friendship.* (London: J. M. Dent & Sons, 1968).

Matthews, T. S., *Great Tom. Notes towards the Definition of T. S. Eliot.* (London: Weidenfeld and Nicolson, 1974).

Moody, A. D., *Thomas Stearns Eliot: Poet* (Cambridge: Cambridge University Press, 1979).

March, Richard, and Tambimuttu (eds.), *T. S. Eliot: A Symposium from C. Aiken, L. Ancesci and Others* (London: Editions Poetry, 1948).

Matthiessen, F. O., *The Achievement of T. S. Eliot* (Oxford: Oxford University Press, 1935).

Menand, Louis, *Discovering Modernism: T.S. Eliot and his Context* (Oxford: Oxford University Press, 1987).

Paulin, Tom, 'Many Cunning Passages', in *Times Literary Supplement* (Nov. 29, 2002), 14–15.

Rainey, Lawrence, *Institutions of Modernism: Literary Elites and Public Culture* (New Haven: Yale University Press, 1998).

—— *The Annotated Waste Land with Eliot's Contemporary Prose* (New Haven: Yale University Press, 2005).

Sencourt, Robert, *T. S. Eliot: A Memoir*, ed. Donald Adamson (London: Garnstone Press, 1971).

Seymour-Jones, Carole, *Painted Shadow: A Life of Vivienne Eliot* (London: Constable, 2001).

Southam, B. C., *A Student's Guide to the Selected Poems of T. S. Eliot* (London: Faber & Faber, 1968; 6th edn., 1994).

Tate, Allen (ed.), *T. S. Eliot: The Man and his Work* (London: Chatto & Windus, 1967).

OTHER WORKS

Aiken, Conrad, *Ushant. An Essay* (Boston: Duell, Sloan and Peace, 1952).

Aldington, Richard, *Stepping Heavenward. A Record* (London: Chatto & Windus, 1931).

Bergson, Henri, *Matter and Memory* (New York: Zone Books, 1988).

Ellmann, Richard, *James Joyce*, Rev. edn. (Oxford: Oxford University Press, 1983).

Freud, Sigmund, *The Complete Psychological Works* (London: Hogarth Press, 1953).

Keynes, J. M., *The Economic Consequences of the Peace* (New York:

Harcourt, Brace and Howe, 1920).

Kuklick, Bruce, *The Rise of American Philosophy: Cambridge, Massachusetts, 1860–1930* (New Haven and London: Yale University Press, 1977).

Leavis, F. R., *New Bearings in English Poetry* (London: Chatto and Windus, 1932).

MacCabe, Colin, *Godard: A Portrait of the Artist at 70* (London: Bloomsbury, 2003).

Marx, Groucho, *The Groucho Letters; Letters from and to Groucho Marx* (New York: Simon and Schuster, 1967).

Monk, Ray, *Bertrand Russell* (London: Jonathan Cape, 1996).

Paris Review; Interview Issue, 21 (Spring/ Summer 1959).

Paulin, Tom, 'Many Cunning Passages', *Times Literary Supplement* (Nov. 29, 2002) 14–15.

Pound, Ezra, *The Spirit of Romance*, Rev. edn. (London: J. M. Dent, 1910).

—— *The Letters of Ezra Pound 1907–1941*, ed. D. D. Paige (London: Faber & Faber, 1951).

Reid, B. L., *The Man from New York. John Quinn and his Friends* (New York: Oxford University Press, 1968).

Sassoon, Siegfried, *Diaries, 1920–22*, ed. and intro. Rupert Hart-Davis (London: Faber & Faber, 1981).

Trotter, David, *Cinema and Modernism* (Oxford: Blackwell, forthcoming).

Williams, Raymond, *Culture and Society, 1780–1950* (New York: Columbia University Press, 1983).

Williams, William Carlos, *The Autobiography of William Carlos Williams* (New York: Random House, 1948).

Wilson, Edmund, *Classics and Commercials: A Literary Chronicle of the Forties* (New York: Farrar, Straus and Giroux, 1950).

Woolf, Leonard, *Beginning Again. An Autobiography of the Years 1911–1918* (London: Hogarth Press, 1964).

Woolf, Virginia, *The Diaries of Virginia Woolf*, ed. Anne Olivier Bell, i–iv (London: Harcourt Brace Jovanovich, 1977, 1978, 1980, 1984).

—— *The Letters of Virginia Woolf*, ed. Nigel Nicolson and Joanna Trautmann, i–vi (London: Harcourt Brace Jovanovich, 1975, 1976, 1977, 1978, 1979, 1980).

Index

Printed in the United Kingdom
by Lightning Source UK Ltd.
116213UKS00001B/175-288